The Quality 75

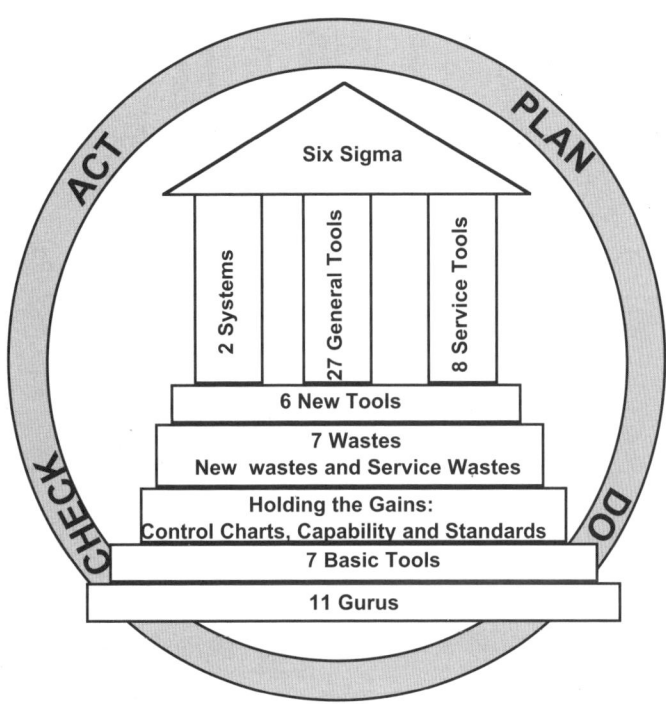

Towards Six Sigma Performance
in Service and Manufacturing

John Bicheno

ISBN 0 9541244 0 5

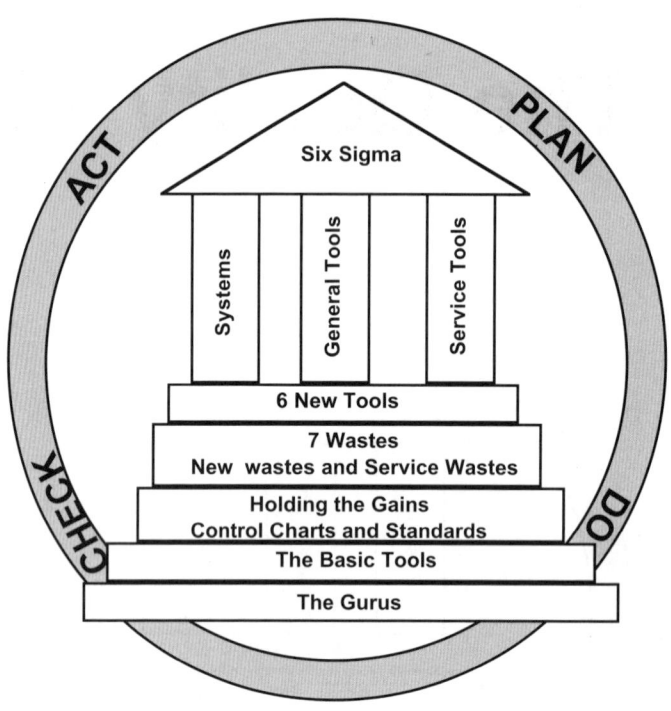

For
Sally, Ann, Heather
and Rusalka

Published by
PICSIE Books
Box 622
Buckingham, MK18 7YE
U.K.

Telephone and fax for orders: +44 (0) 1280 815023

e mail: picsie@axiom.co.uk
website: www.picsie.co.uk

Copyright © 1991, 1994, 1998, 2001. Publication date January 2002
All rights reserved.
Revised edition August 2002
Printed by Moreton Press. Telephone 01280 818918

A British Library Cataloguing-in-Publication Data.
A catalogue record for this book is available from the British Library

Contents

The Tools and PDCA and EFQM 4,5
The Gurus
Deming 7
Juran 9
Crosby 12
Feigenbaum 13
Ishikawa 14
Garvin 16
Shingo (Failsafing and Quality at Source) 17
Taguchi 18
Kano 20
Grönroos 22
Shainin and Bhote 23

Improvement Cycles
PDCA 25
DMAIC 26

7 Tools
Process Mapping 29
Pareto Analysis 30
Fishbone Diagram 31
Histogram and Measles Chart 31
Run Diagram (Multi-Vari Chart) 32
Correlation and Stratification 33
Check Sheets and Tally Chart 34
(Cross Impact Analysis) 34

Holding the Gains
Statistical Process Control (SPC) 37
Process Capability 40
Standards and Standard Operating Procedures 42

Six New Tools
Affinity Diagram 45
Interrelationship and Network Diagram 46
Tree Diagram 47
Contingency Chart 47
Matrix Analysis 48
Critical Path Analysis 50

7 Wastes
Overproduction 53
Waiting 54
Transporting 54
Inappropriate Processing 54
Unnecessary Inventory 55
Unnecessary Motion 55
Defects 55
New Wastes 56
Service Wastes 56

General Tools
5S (or CANDO) 59
5 Whys and Root Cause Analysis 61
6 Honest Serving Men & Is-Is Not 62
Benchmarking 63
Best Demonstrated Practice 65
Blitz 66
Better Brainstorming 68
Cost of Quality 68
Cusums 70
Data Display 71
Defects per Million (DPMO) 72
Design of Experiments (DOE) 73
Disruptive Technologies 75
Failure Modes & Effect Analysis (FMEA) 76
Force Field Analysis 77
Hoshin 78
Importance Performance Matrix 80
Johari Window 81
Kaizen 82
Market Survey 84
Nominal Group Technique (NGT) 85
Precontrol 87
Process Model and PETS 88
Quality Function Deployment (QFD) 88
Single Point Lessons 92
Supplier Partnership 93
Sustainability 95

Service Tools
Cycle of Service and Customer Processing 99
Moments of Truth 100
Service Blueprinting 101
Loyalty 103
Service Gaps and SERVQUAL 106
Service Profit Chain 108
Service Recovery, Retention, 3R's 109
Zone of Tolerance 111

Systems
ISO 9001:2000 113
EFQM Excellence Model 115

Six Sigma 119

PDCA, DMAIC and Tools

PDCA	DMAIC			Tools
Plan	Define	What is the problem?	Identify Opportunities / Scope the Project	Benchmarking, QFD, Disruptive Tech, Hoshin, FMEA, Serv Gaps, Pareto, Importance Performance, Cost of Quality, Market survey Tree Diagram, Critical Path Anal, Mapping, NGT, Best Demo Prac
	Measure	How are we doing?	Analyse the Process / Define Outcomes	7 tools, DPMO, Data Presentation, Process Chain, 5 Whys, MoT, Kano 6 Honest Men, Supplier Partners Capability analysis, CoQ Maps, Blueprints, SERVQUAL
	Analyse	What is wrong?	Identify Root Causes	5 Whys, FMEA, 7 tools, DOE, QFD, Matrix analysis, Shainin Gap analysis, Benchmarking, Zone of tolerance, Cusum
Do	Improve	Fix it	Prioritise / Refine / Implement	QFD, Matrix analysis, Hoshin QFD, Affinity, Contingency, FMEA Force Field, Kaizen, Blitz Critical path Single point lessons, Johari
Check / Act	Control	Hold the gains. Celebrate.	Measure outcomes / Acknowledge	Control Charts and SPC, 5S Standardisation, DPMO, Cusum Cost of Quality, ISO 9001:2000, Sustainability, Capability, Supplier Partnership

EFQM and Tools

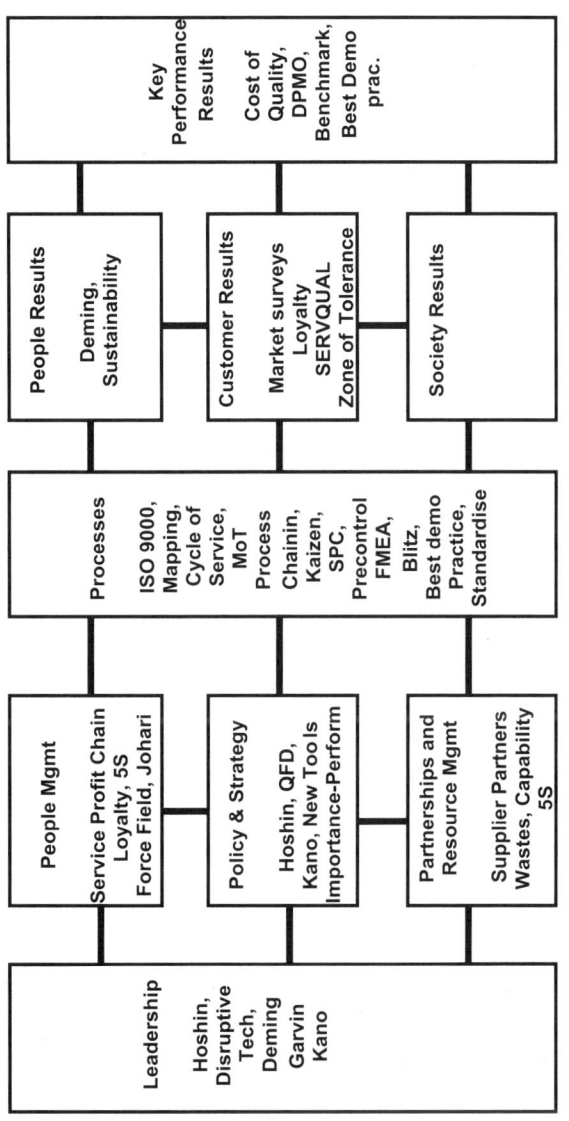

Copyright EFQM 1999. The EFQM Excellence Model is a registered trademark and reproduced with permission of the EFQM

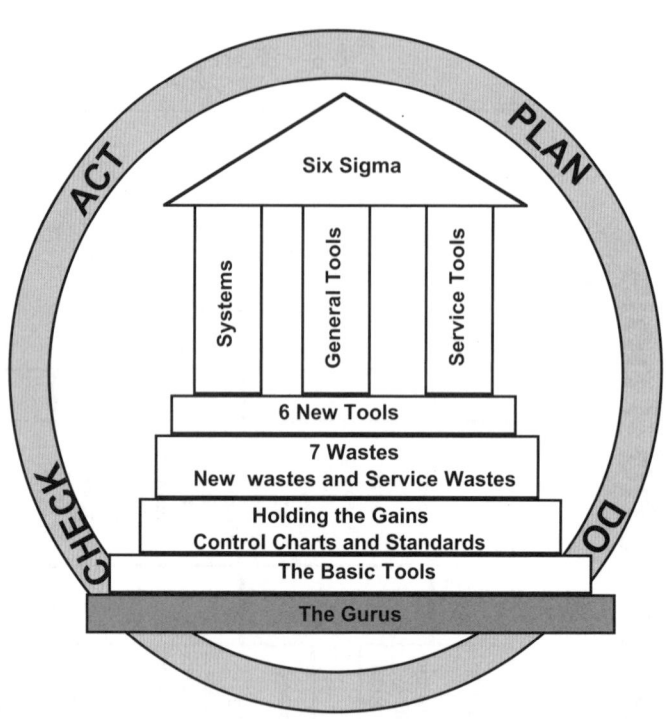

The Gurus

Deming
Juran
Crosby
Feigenbaum
Ishikawa

Garvin

Shingo
Taguchi
Kano
Grönroos
Shainin and Bhote

The Gurus

The field of Quality Management has been strongly influenced by a number of "Gurus". Any choice of which Gurus to include would certainly include the first four given below, but beyond that opinions differ. In any case, it would be a mistake to concentrate solely on the views of one Guru. All have useful things to say. The reader has to distil out those views that are most appropriate to his or her organization.

Deming

Dr. W. Edwards Deming (1900-1993) is probably the most revered figure in quality management. In the 1950s, Deming taught quality to the Japanese by insisting that top management attend his courses. They did, and prospered. Originally Deming taught statistical process control (SPC) to the Japanese and has always maintained that management must have an appreciation of statistical variation. Today Deming is mainly associated with quality management theories, particularly his "14 point" plan, the "Deming Cycle" and his "deadly diseases".

In his *System of Profound Knowledge* Deming has four interrelating theories: The *Theory of Systems* recognises that everything is interconnected. A holistic approach is necessary. The *Theory of Variation* recognises that variation is endemic. Management's failure to account for variation in managing everything was one of Deming's great criticisms. The *Theory of Knowledge* studies the way in which we experiment and learn. *The Theory of Psychology* is considered by Deming to be fundamental to understanding people and teams. What is amazing is that these four are amongst the most fashionable ideas in management today - 40 years plus after Deming - but are still usually treated in isolation.

Appreciation of statistical variation begins with the concept that very little in life is absolutely consistent, and that chance will account for a certain amount of "natural variation". So, for example, a salesman cannot sell exactly the same amount every month. He would have good and bad months, and the differences between good and bad are mainly explained by chance rather than by variations in the salesman's skills. Therefore merely to reward him for the good months, and to penalize for the bad could be de-motivating and poor management. On the other hand truly superior performance can produce sales which are significantly and consistently better. Here, special reward would be justified as would penalties in the case of consistently poor performance.

To illustrate the point, Deming used to do a famous experiment - the "red bead game". Five players are picked from the audience. Each is given a paddle with slots into which coloured beads fit. The players are asked to dip the paddles into a bowl containing a mix of white and red beads. The object is to get as few red beads (representing defectives) as possible. Of course, it is nearly impossible to get zero red. But the numbers of red beads varies between the players. Deming commends the player with the smallest number of reds and admonishes the player with the most reds. This is typical management behaviour according to Deming. More rounds are played, sometimes resulting in one of the players getting "fired" and others where the raise awarded to the best players "goes to his head". The audience quickly grasps the futility of paying for performance when the process is not under the player's control. The messages are that management must understand variation, and that improving the process, not motivation, is critical for success.

Common causes are inherent in the process but special causes are not, and these special causes need to be identified. Poor sales is one example but the same would apply to many other areas of both human-based and machine-based performance. (For machines, this is the basis of SPC.) Moreover, true performance improvement is very seldom within the sole power of an operator or salesman or supervisor. For example, a machine has natural variation and may be producing a certain percentage of defects. The operator can do little about it. Without management action or support significant improvement can seldom be made. Deming's rule of thumb is that perhaps 85% of improvement requires management effort, while only 15% is actionable solely by front line employees. So, mere exhortations and incentives to produce better quality will have only limited results. "Be guided by theory" was a favourite saying.

Defining Quality

Deming said that quality can only be defined in terms of customer satisfaction. Thus there is no absolute measure - two customers may perceive a product or service quality differently. Hence it is management's task to translate the future needs of customers into quality products and services.

The 14 Points

It is sobering to realise that many ideas which are regarded as new and fashionable today were recommended by Deming over 30 years ago. These include continuous improvement (Kaizen) (see point 5 of the 14 points and the PDCA cycle), business process reengineering (see point 9), supplier partnership (point 4), self directed work teams (point 7), and Hoshin (point 1). Perhaps there are more ideas whose time is yet to come! Deming's 14 point plan is a complete philosophy of management, not just quality management. Books have been written on the subject. Here we attempt a brief summary.

1. There should be a consistent message about quality, throughout the organization. It should not vary by department, by pressure of work, by time of the month, or by customer. Usually a clear statement is required from management, with actions that demonstrate that it means what is says.
2. The new age of quality requires a commitment continuously to improve. The competition is doing this; so must you in order to survive. Customers have increasing expectations about quality.
3. Switch from defect detection to defect prevention. Rather inspect the process than the product. Work to understand and reduce the natural variation in processes. The less the variation, the better.
4. In dealing with suppliers, end the practice of awarding business on price. Move towards quality of product, reliability of delivery, and willingness to cooperate and improve. In other words build partnerships with suppliers. There should be advantages for both parties.
5. Constantly improve. Use the PDCA cycle. (See separate section). Improvement is not confined to products and their direct processes, but to all supporting services and activities also.
6. Train in a modern way. Let employees understand the concept of variation, basic SPC, improvement, and the total approach to quality. The idea is to make everyone responsible for their own quality.
7. Supervision must change from chasing to coaching and support.
8. "Drive out fear" of improvement. Management must create the environment which removes all possibility that improvement in quality will somehow penalize operators, through more work, loss of jobs, financial loss, or whatever.
9. Remove any organizational barrier that prevents quality improvement. This means improved visibility between sections and also easier communications. Aim to remove any barrier that prevents the requirements and reactions of the customer being moved rapidly and without distortion to the point where action can be taken.
10. Don't have slogans that mean nothing. Don't have unrealistic targets. Remember, management has most of the power to make real improvements.
11. Deming's eleventh point maintains that work standards and numerical quotas should be eliminated. This is controversial, unless interpreted with the understanding of natural variation. Natural variation says that no standard or quota can be exact and without variation. If the natural variation is understood, the quotas and standards that are beyond the control of employees should not be penalized (nor rewarded for undeserved performance.)
12. Remove barriers that prevent employees having pride in their work. These barriers may include unrealistic quotas and time pressure, short-term requirements for profit rather than quality, lack of investment in the right machines or tools, individual incentive schemes based on

output rather than group based schemes based on quality and improvement, and lack of management support or consistency.

13. Train and educate. This follows from point 6 but emphasises that education must be widely based and continuing. Despite being point number 13, it is usually the starting point, after point 1.
14. Create an organizational structure that will support all the previous points. This is important because the 14 point plan is not a short term implementation, but rather a long term philosophy.

The Deming Cycle (or PDCA cycle)

The Deming Cycle is a powerful concept that has picked up several variations. This important topic is described in a separate section.

The "Deadly Diseases"

The seven "deadly diseases" of quality, as Deming terms them, amount to a severe criticism of Western management and organizational practices. The first five are closely related. They are worth pondering, and re-pondering:

1. "Lack of constancy of purpose" is a disease that appears in Deming's 14 point plan. It is a reminder about inconsistent policy on quality, particularly as the end-of-period rush begins! A twin point is,
2. "Emphasis on short term profits" is a reminder to take a more consistent view, without being influenced by the end-of-period financial performance. And this may be brought about by the next point.
3. Overemphasis on performance appraisal and merit rating, particularly when judged solely on financial performance. In an earlier section the issue of variation was discussed. If variation is not understood, appraisal can be literally destructive. He said that America had become great through teamwork, not competition. Deming was particularly worried by the emphasis on short term results rather than on coaching and helping staff to develop their potential. This is made worse by the next two diseases.
4. Too much staff mobility, where managers do not get to learn the real problems and requirements of an organization.
5. Overdependence on figures, particularly financial, which can be massaged to look good in the short term, while the longer term suffers.
6 and 7. The last two points relate to excessive medical costs and excessive legal costs, which Deming believes are paralysing competitiveness. Some would regard these as being typically American problems, but they may be a foretaste of problems to come for others.

Further reading on Deming

W Edwards Deming, *Out of the Crisis*, Cambridge University Press, 1982

W Edwards Deming, *Quality, Productivity, and Competitive Position*, MIT Centre for Advanced Engineering Study, 1982

W.J.Latzko and W.J. Saunders, *Four Days with Dr. Deming*, Addison Wesley, Reading, MA, 1995

Web sites:
www.deming.org
www.deming.eng.clemson.edu
www.michiganquality.org

Juran

Like Deming, Dr. Joseph Juran is given credit for developing Japanese quality in the 1950s. His books on quality since then have had a profound influence around the world, and are so wide ranging it is difficult to highlight particular contributions from the many that have been made. Perhaps the best known Juran concepts are his definitions of quality, the concepts of "breakthrough" and the "internal customer", and the "quality trilogy". Juran also was responsible for "Pareto analysis" as applied to problem solving, for work on the costing of quality, and for the idea of a "Quality Council" within the organization. Juran has now retired from public lectures, although he continues writing. At the time of writing he is in his late 90's.

Juran believes that there are two dimensions to quality, an external one concerned with matching customer requirements, and an internal one concerned with building the product or service correctly. Juran has proposed the well known definition of quality as "fitness for use". This is not as simple as it sounds. One needs to ask, "for whose use?", and "what is the real use?". There may be many possible customers, both internal and external, who may use the product in different ways. (More on external customers later.) So quality begins with a close understanding of who the users will be and how and where the product will be used. Without this customer orientation, good quality is not possible.

Using some JURAN concepts

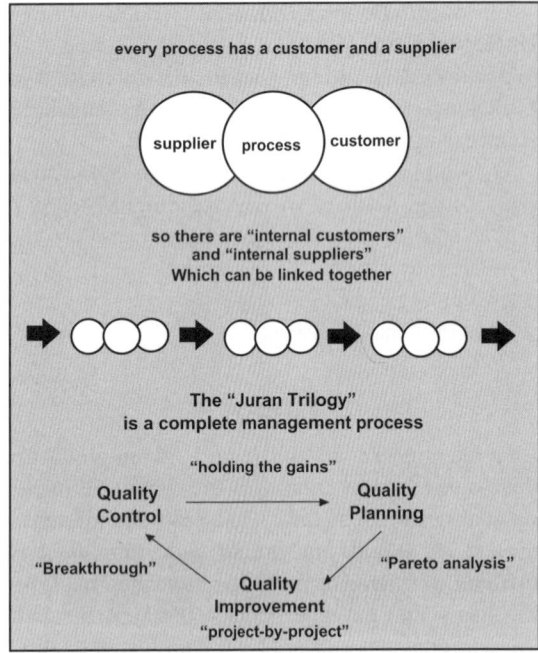

And what is an "internal customer"? Each person along the chain, from product design to final user is both a supplier and a customer. Also, of course, the person will be a "process", carrying out some transformation or activity. The process is subject to all the concepts of process control. Taking them together, this is what Juran refers to as the "three role model", that is, each stage is a supplier, a process, and customer or user. So the customer orientation mentioned earlier applies internally as well. At each stage there is opportunity to improve the product, perhaps making it easier to handle, or fit together, or maintain, or update.

Juran emphasises the necessity for ongoing quality improvement. He maintains that this is only achieved through "project by project" improvement, in other words by a succession of small improvement projects carried out throughout the organization. Projects may be suggested by management, by operators (perhaps through quality circles), by quality specialists or by Pareto analysis of existing problems. Juran was the first to name the Pareto principle and to describe it as a universal problem solving methodology. The Pareto principle simply sets out to identify the "vital few" as opposed to the "trivial many" or the "useful many". This is the well known phenomenon that there will always be a relatively few processes or people or defects or problems that somehow take up most of the time or effort or cost. Hence it makes sense to identify these and to tackle them first. (Pareto analysis is one of the 7 tools - see that section for more detail.)

Improvement projects can also be identified through costs, and Juran was responsible for suggesting that quality costs (or the costs of not getting something right first time) should be recorded and classified. Money is the prime language of management, so that if the costs of poor quality are known this not only gets management attention but helps home in on where effort should be made. For Juran, it is necessary for middle managers in the quality area to be able to translate the language of things into the language of money and vice versa. To do this we need a classification system, and Juran suggested that quality costs could be grouped into failure or appraisal or prevention costs. See the section on Cost of Quality.

Juran emphasized that management needs to attack the "chronic" underlying poor quality that is often not even recognised. He says that there is a tendency to tackle only "sporadic" quality problems that surface from time to time. Breakthrough is needed. The way to tackle chronic quality problems is "project by project improvement". This is perhaps similar to the Deming cycle, and leads straight into the quality trilogy. The quality trilogy, according to Juran comprises quality planning, quality control, and quality improvement. These can be seen as being parallel to the financial processes of budgeting, cost control, and cost reduction. Good quality management requires the quality actions to be planned out, improved, and controlled. So the process can be seen as achieving control at one level of quality performance, then planning to be better, project by project using the tools and techniques discussed, then eventually achieving "breakthrough" to an improved level, and then once again controlling at the new level. This series of actions will not take place by chance or by a series of uncoordinated actions. Rather, they must be organized in a systematic way. This is where the "Quality Council" comes in. This body, typically comprising senior managers, has the responsibility for coordinating the quality improvement actions and projects. They would, for example, set goals, identify needs, establish training, ensure measurements (such as costs of quality), undertake coordination, and in general liaise between quality projects and top management.

In another parallel with the Deming cycle, the Juran breakthrough sequence sees the improvement process as taking two "journeys" - the "journey from symptom to cause" and the "journey from cause to remedy". The first journey moves one from the problem to the "diagnosis" and may be seen as parallel to the "P" and "D" stages of the Deming cycle. Here we are concerned with identification, using for example Pareto, and with the generation of and testing of hypotheses to find the contributing causes. The second journey moves one from the "diagnosis" to the "solution" and may be seen as parallel to the "C" and "A" stages of the Deming cycle. Here one makes the selection of the appropriate cause, implements the necessary actions, and then replicates the improvements where possible in other areas.

Juran has also written on product design. His "Road Map" has 9 junctions: identify customers, determine the needs of those customers, translate those needs into company language, develop a product that can respond to those needs, optimise the product's features to meet both company needs and customer needs, develop a process that is capable of producing the product, optimise the process, prove that the process can produce the product under operating conditions, and transfer the process to operations.

More recently, Juran has spoken about "Big Q". This is to emphasize that quality is not just the concern of production or even of total quality within the organization, but extends further into the linkage between organizations, and includes all service organizations and operations. Under Big Q the concept of "customer" extends beyond those immediately involved with producing and using the product or service, to include stakeholders who have a legitimate concern such as legislators and consumer groups. Juran states "In many companies there is only a dim awareness that the scope of the customer has widened, so there is no longer a consensus on who is the customer".

Finally in his last (edited) fascinating book covering the history of quality, Juran expresses his views on the future of managing for quality. He sees a parallel with the field of finance and accounting where, for example, the field is organised into distinct processes such as auditing, standard reports have been developed which are widely read and used by top managers, key terms are in widespread use, there are professional examinations, national indexes have been developed, awareness of the importance of the area will be recognized by legislators and economists, and the subject is taught in school.

Further reading:
Joseph Juran and A. Blanton Godfrey, *Quality Control Handbook*, Fifth edition, McGraw Hill, 1999. (The bible on quality!)
Joseph Juran, *Juran on Planning for Quality*, The Free Press, 1988
J.M. Juran, *Juran on Leadership for Quality*, The Free Press, 1989
J.M. Juran (ed), *A History of Managing for Quality*, ASQ Quality Press, 1995
John Butman, *Juran : A Lifetime of Influence*, Wiley, New York, 1997
Web site (The Juran Institute, containing news and recent articles) : www.juran.com

Crosby

Like Juran, Phil Crosby has been a prolific writer on quality. Unlike Juran, some of whose works contain much quantitative and statistical techniques, Crosby concentrates on quality philosophy, particularly relating to management. Crosby's dynamic speaking style and stimulating writing style have gained him a large following.

Crosby is perhaps best known for his "four absolutes" of quality, his phrase "quality is free", his 14 point plan (different from Deming's 14 points), and his down to earth common sense on a wide range of quality topics.

Crosby's "four absolutes" are :

1. "The definition of quality is conformance to requirements". This very specific definition of quality leaves very little open, which is probably what Crosby intends. According to Crosby, once the requirements are specified then quality is judged solely on the criteria of whether they are met or not; aesthetics or feelings don't come into it. It is then the duty of management to specify those requirements very clearly, to say what they want. This, Crosby believes, is one of the major failings of management. Of course, if management does not decide what is needed then by default, operators are going to have to make that decision for the company!

2. "The system of quality is prevention". In other words, prevention is better than detection or appraisal. This is very much in line with the philosophy behind SPC and failsafing; understand the process, look at what can go wrong, and take preventative actions.

3. "The performance standard is zero defect", or "ZD" as Crosby calls it. Here Crosby is stating that nothing less than perfect quality has to be the aim. Setting targets below 100% is the start of a downward spiral. Of course, traditional quality management has taken zero defects to be uneconomic, and there should be a trade-off between prevention costs and failure costs. The Crosby view is now supported by a developing view that prevention costs, particularly where "total quality" is in place, do not necessarily rise massively as one approaches zero defects, but in fact rise by no more than failure costs fall. In other words, zero defect may well be optimal from a cost point of view. But again it comes back to getting the requirements right in the first place.

4. "The measurement of quality is the price of nonconformance". Like Juran, Crosby believes in costing quality as a prime motivator for management. Crosby classifies costs into "PONC" - the price of nonconformance" (all the costs involved in not getting the product or service right) and "POC" - the price of conformance (what it costs to do things right; prevention, detection, etc.). Here Crosby's famous phrase "quality is free" is appropriate. (It is also the title of his first book.) As he says, "it's not a gift, but it's free" or in other words if you put effort into improving quality it will more than pay for itself through improved productivity, reduced rework and claims, and improved customer satisfaction.

The problem with quality, according to Crosby, is not that people disagree with it, but what they think they know about it, namely that workers are sloppy, customers are unreasonable, close checks will find problems earlier, and that there are "trade-offs" in quality. In 1995 Crosby concluded that, after a brief period of improvement, these ideas are once again gaining ground.

Crosby, like Deming, has a 14 step plan for quality improvement. Deming's 14 points are more of a philosophy of quality management, whereas Crosby's are more a specific action plan for implementation. In that respect, the two 14 point plans can easily be seen as reinforcing one another. The 14 steps will not be spelled out in detail here, but they begin with management commitment and the establishment of a team. The next stages deal with measuring quality through "POC" and "PONC". These figures are often much higher than expected, which aids in the next steps to do with creating awareness and planning out what is to be done. Education of employees follows, with a "ZD" day to launch the program. Then employees become involved in detail goal setting as to what can be done in specific sections of the company. With the goals set, identification of the causes of defects can begin in earnest at all levels. Improvement results and recognition must then be given. Now "quality councils" allow quality managers and others to get together and review what has been achieved and how and where else these achievements can be transferred to. This is not the end. Quality is an ongoing process, so the last step is to do it all over again.

Writing years later, Crosby now regrets putting forward his 14 point plan, making the point that many take it as a recipe for quality when what is really required is appropriate thought ("searching for specific procedures among ideas is the sign of a lazy mind"), but that such frameworks should be added to through experience, study and reflection.

Crosby's "Quality Vaccine" is perhaps more closely related to the Deming 14 point plan than the Crosby 14 step process. In typical stimulating style, Crosby's "vaccine" is preventive medicine for management against poor quality. The vaccine comprises practical advice on 21 areas, subdivided into five sections. The quality vaccine is in fact a succinct summary of what is needed for total quality management.

* The first section deals with integrity. This is really about taking quality seriously, from chief executive to every employee. If quality is taken as "first among equals" - the others being marketing, finance, operations, and so on, then everyone understands that their own future and the future of the company will be determined by performance on quality.
* The second section deals with systems - for quality costs, for education, for quality performance, for review and improvement, and for customer satisfaction. All of these must be designed and put in place.
* The third section deals with the need for communication and for communication systems that will make clear the requirements and specifications, and which will communicate improvement opportunities within the organization. Crosby often emphasises the importance of listening - to customers, and to those front line employees who often know what is needed but perhaps have never been asked. Also external communications, in advertising, letters, and product information must convey a consistent message.
* The fourth section deals with operations, including working with and developing suppliers. Processes must be prepared prior to use and made capable, and process improvement must become the norm.
* And last, Crosby maintains that policies must be made clear and consistent throughout the organization.

Crosby also has a "Quality Management Maturity Grid" passing through the stages of uncertainty, awakening, enlightenment, and wisdom and certainty. During this transition the reported typical cost of quality as a percentage of sales, starts unknown, rises to 8%, then declines to 2.5%. But the actual costs of quality declines from 20% to 2.5%.

In recent years Crosby has been critical of ISO 9000 and of quality awards such as the Baldridge or EQA, saying that they are old fashioned, merely providing a living for consultants, and a recipe for managers who don't want to think about what quality really is! Phil Crosby died in August 2001.

Further reading on Crosby
Phil Crosby, *Quality is Free*, McGraw Hill, 1979
Phil Crosby, *Quality Without Tears*, McGraw Hill, 1984
Phil Crosby, *Let's Talk Quality*, McGraw Hill, 1989
Phil Crosby, *Quality is Still Free*, McGraw Hill, 1995

Web site
www.philipcrosby.com

Feigenbaum

Armand Feigenbaum, an American engineer, was the originator of "Total Quality Control", now often referred to simply as total quality. In the 1950s, he defined total quality as follows :

"Total quality control is an effective system for integrating the quality development, quality maintenance, and quality improvement efforts of the various groups in an organization so as to enable production and service at the most economical levels which allow full customer satisfaction."

Feigenbaum has a particularly good definition of quality: "The total composite product and service characteristics of marketing, engineering, manufacture and maintenance through which the product and service in use will meet the expectations of the customer."

Feigenbaum referred to the "industrial cycle" which is the ongoing sequence of activities necessary to bring products from concept to market. Included in this cycle are marketing, design, engineering, purchasing, manufacturing, production, inspection, packaging and shipping, installation, and service. In all these stages quality has requirements to be met. Feigenbaum was the first to point out the folly of regarding quality professionals as being solely responsible for the quality function. The cycle begins and ends with the customer, but in between many people and functions must play a role; in fact everyone has a role and the responsibility must be shared. On the other hand Feigenbaum sees the quality professionals playing a central role and coordinating the entire process. He does not appear to agree with the view of quality improvement being a required role for all employees. As one moves through the cycle, there are requirements to be met at each stage, and these different requirements must be defined and communicated. This is where the quality professionals have a prime role. The total cost of quality (or non quality) accumulates through all these stages, and a total view of quality being managed through all the stages will lead to a lower overall cost.

Feigenbaum has a 40 point plan for quality which is far more detailed and specific that those of Deming or Crosby. (See the web site for a full listing). In general he has 3 steps to Quality : quality leadership, modern quality technology, and organisational commitment.

Feigenbaum is also known for his concept of the "hidden plant". That is that in every factory a certain proportion of its capacity is wasted through not getting it right first time. Feigenbaum quoted a figure of up to 40% of the capacity of the plant being wasted. At the time this was an unbelievable figure; even today some managers are still to learn that this is a figure not too far removed from the truth.

Further reading:
A.V. Feigenbaum, "Total Quality Control", *Harvard Business Review*, November 1956
Armand Feigenbaum, *Total Quality Control*, (Third Edition, revised) McGraw Hill, 1991

Web sites: www.generalsystemscompany.com

Ishikawa

The late Kaoru Ishikawa is regarded as the leading Japanese contributor to quality management. His contributions are extensive but perhaps the most noteworthy are his development of the total quality viewpoint, his work on statistical quality control, his emphasis on the human side of quality, and his invention of the Ishikawa diagram and the use of the "7 tools". Perhaps most noteworthy is the fact that he is widely regarded as the "father" of quality circles, since it was he who furthered the concept of circles and popularized their practice in Japan.

Ishikawa extended the total quality view of Feigenbaum by suggesting that operators, and employees in general, have a greater role to play in all the stages suggested by Feigenbaum. In fact, Ishikawa believed that although the total quality view was invented in the West, its potential was limited there due to over-reliance on quality professionals and insufficient attention to the contribution that everyone can make. This leads directly onto quality circles and to his classification of statistical tools for quality control.

Ishikawa classified statistical quality control techniques into three groups of increasing complexity. The first group is the classic "7 tools" (dealt with in a complete separate section), which require minimal statistical knowledge. (The 7 tools include the Ishikawa or fishbone diagram, which is described in that section.) Ishikawa believed that the 7 tools should be known widely, if not by everyone, in the company. They are certainly not the preserve of experts, and are simple enough for everyone to use for ongoing improvement. More specifically they should be used by quality circle members in analysing problems and devising improvements. Used together, they form a powerful set. The next group ("intermediate statistical methods"), are for use by quality specialists but also by some managers who have responsibilities for quality in their sections. Not all these managers need to know about all these methods. They include sampling surveys and sampling inspection, statistical estimation and hypothesis testing, sensory tests, and basic experimental design. These methods do require some prior knowledge of statistics but can and should be learned by relevant managers. Lastly there are some "advanced statistical methods" which are primarily for the use of specialist quality staff and consultants. These include advanced experimental design, multivariate analysis, and operations research techniques. (Note: this would include "Taguchi" methods which are discussed in a later section.)

The classification is a useful "Pareto" type of listing. First, it provides general guidance on how an educational program for quality may be set up. Second, Ishikawa believed that most quality problems - perhaps 90% or more - could be solved by the use of the 7 tools category, and that therefore they should be known to all, from company chief executive right through to operator. Ishikawa has perhaps been more instrumental than anyone in the now widely held Japanese view that without at least some knowledge of statistics, quality management is not possible. Going back to Deming's view on variation, one can notice the similarity.

Ishikawa insisted that "total quality" implies participation by everyone in the organization. Moreover, it is achieved through everyone participating in teams rather than as individuals. In this respect he talks about quality being a "thought revolution". He is critical of heavy dependence on Taylorism which he believed dehumanizes the workplace and destroys much of the opportunity for improvement. (Quality is based on "respect for humanity".) It takes time to build the necessary widespread human commitment and, according to Ishikawa, too rapid implementation of systems such as total quality and just-in-time is the reason why they have often not been a success. Quality is not a "miracle drug" but rather a "herb medicine". Despite Ishikawa's heavy inclination towards people involvement, this should not be misread as a willingness to avoid quantitative data. On the contrary, Ishikawa is adamant that collection and analysis of the hard facts and data is the essence of quality control. Hence everyone must be trained in basic tools and statistical techniques.

Ishikawa believed that quality begins with the customer. The essence is to understand customers, their requirements, what they can afford, and what their reactions are likely to be. Absolute clarity of specification is needed, and this means specifying exactly what is needed under what conditions, of for example temperature and humidity. He believed that customer complaints are a vital quality improvement opportunity, and that they must be managed. In this respect Ishikawa was the pioneer of the fashionable idea that customer complaints must be actively encouraged.

Ishikawa's quality philosophy is summarised in his 11 points which are :
1. Quality begins and ends with education.
2. The first step is to know customer requirements.
3. The ideal state is when inspection is no longer necessary.
4. Remove the root cause, not the symptoms.
5. Quality is the responsibility of all.
6. Do not confuse means with objectives.
7. Put quality first to achieve long term profits.
8. Marketing is the entrance and exit of quality.
9. Top management should not be angered by facts shown by subordinates.
10. 95% of problems can be solved with simple tools.
11. Data without variability is false data.

On the perennial question of whether quality pays, Ishikawa believes that it does, provided one defines the relevant system wide enough. In other words if quality is equated with inspection then perfection may not be worthwhile. But if quality incorporates the total process, from customer to design and through process control and eventually back to the customer, then it certainly pays.

Finding the root causes of problems was important to Ishikawa, and of course his famous Ishikawa diagram assists in this respect.

As noted, Ishikawa is regarded as the "father" of quality circles. Of course he has extensive advice on how to conduct circles, but a few points are noteworthy. Primarily, circle activities must be part of a wider total quality effort. Managers must first understand both total quality and the functioning of circles before circle activities begin. Those supervisors in whose areas circles are in operation require special training. Members of a circle must be volunteers, but on the other hand everyone in a section has a role to play in quality. So it is an all or nothing affair. Circle members must be trained in appropriate tools, but must also learn to appreciate wider aspects of quality throughout the organization. The organization must cater for these requirements. A problem solving methodology must be learned by team members (Ishikawa's has 9 steps, but can be seen as similar to the Deming cycle.) Effective evaluation of circle efforts must be made. Perhaps one can summarize the Ishikawa approach with his well known axiom - that management must conduct their programs with a "belief in humanity".

Further reading:
Kaoru Ishikawa, *Guide to Quality Control*, Asian Productivity Association, 1976
Kaoru Ishikawa, *What is Total Quality Control? The Japanese Way,* Prentice Hall, 1985

Garvin

David Garvin, a professor at Harvard Business School, has contributed to the concept of quality as a strategy, and to our understanding of just what is meant by quality. Garvin identifies eight "dimensions" of quality, which he maintains cover the various meanings of quality that managers, operators, and customers have. The important idea is that a product or service does not usually compete on all eight, but usually targets only a select few. Likewise customers may have different perceptions as to what combination of the dimensions really add up to a "quality" package. This implies that management must seek to understand customer perceptions, so that quality efforts will be focused. Also there may be opportunities to compete on different or additional dimensions that are not offered by competitors. The eight dimensions are:

1. **Performance**: the primary operating characteristics of the product or service. Examples would be size, speed, power, sound.
2. **Features**: the "extras" that supplement the main performance characteristics. The "sunroof and spotlamps".
3. **Reliability**: what may go wrong and how often it is likely to.
4. **Conformance:** the closeness of match between the design specification and what is actually produced (or the match between what is advertised and what is experienced by customers).
5. **Durability:** how long the product may last, and its robustness in operating conditions. How often service is needed is also relevant.
6. **Serviceability:** the ease, speed, cost and friendliness of service. Whereas reliability is concerned with mean time between failures (MTBF), serviceability is concerned with mean time to repair (MTTR).
7. **Aesthetics**: the appearance, style, "class" and impression.
8. **Perceived Quality**: the "feel", the "finish", and perhaps the reputation. Also the friendliness and the manner in which the customer is served.

Not all dimensions are applicable in the service sector and often other dimensions may be added or substituted. These could include friendliness, helpfulness, clarity of communication, knowledge, safety and security, decision making ability, and response time.

The dimensions are useful because they help understand the breadth of the challenge which is involved in managing quality. In marketing, there is the well known "marketing mix", the point being that product, price, place, and promotion need to be made compatible as a single package. There is apparently also a "quality mix" which requires the same degree of care in its formulation.

Of late, Garvin has become a Guru on the fashionable topic of organisational learning - surely a field closely related to continuous improvement.

Further reading:
David Garvin, *Managing Quality*, The Free Press, 1988

Shingo: Failsafing and Source Inspection

The late Shigeo Shingo is strongly associated with Just-in-Time manufacturing and may not be classified as a quality guru by all. Nevertheless his work on so-called "pokayoke" or fail-safe devices and on "source inspection" is very significant and is already widely implemented. For this reason he is bound to be considered as one of the "greats" sooner or later.

Shigeo Shingo did not invent failsafing ("pokayoke" in Japanese, literally mistake proofing), but developed and classified the concept, particularly in manufacturing. More recently failsafing in services has developed. Shingo's book *Zero Quality Control : Source Inspection and the Pokayoke System* is the classic work.

A failsafing device is a simple, often inexpensive, device which literally prevents defects from being made. The characteristics of a failsafing device are that it undertakes 100% automatic inspection (a true pokayoke would not rely on human memory or action), and either stops or gives warning when a defect is discovered. Note that a pokayoke is not a control device like a thermostat or toilet control valve that takes action every time, but rather a device that senses abnormalities and takes action only when an abnormality is identified.

Shingo distinguishes between "mistakes" (which are inevitable) and "defects" (which result when a mistake reaches a customer.). The aim of pokayoke is to design devices which prevent mistakes becoming defects. Shingo also saw quality control as a hierarchy of effectiveness from "judgment inspection" (where inspectors inspect), to "informative inspection" where information is used to control the process as in SPC, and finally to "source inspection" which aims at checking operating conditions "before the fact". Good pokayokes fall into this last category.

According to Shingo there are three types of failsafing device: "contact", "fixed value", and "motion step", and two actions, control or warning. This means that there are six categories, as shown in the figure with service examples.

The contact type makes contact with every product or has a physical shape which inhibits mistakes. An example is a fixed diameter hole through which all products must fall; an oversize product does not fall through and a defect is registered. The fixed value method is a design which makes it clear when a part is missing or not used. An example is an "egg tray" used for the supply of parts. Sometimes this type can be combined with the contact type, where parts not only have to be present in the egg tray but also are automatically correctly aligned. The motion step type automatically ensures that the correct number of steps have been taken. For example, an operator is required to step on a pressure-sensitive pad during every assembly cycle, or a medicine bottle has a press-down-and-turn feature for safety. Other examples are a checklist, or a correct sequence for switches which do not work unless the order is correct.

Shingo further developed failsafe classification by saying that there are five areas that have potential for failsafing : the operator (Me), the Material, the Machine, the Method, and the Information (4 M plus I). An alternative is the process control model comprising input, process, output, feedback, and result. All are candidates for failsafing. According to Grout (see website), areas where pokayoke should be considered include areas where worker vigilance is required, where mispositioning is likely, where SPC is difficult, where external failure costs dramatically exceed internal failure costs, and in mixed model and

JIT production. Chase and Stewart list four types of pokayoke: Physical (a part can only be used one way), Sequencing (unless the correct steps are carried out it will stop), Grouping (e.g. egg boxes), and Information (e.g. alarm clocks, heijunka boards, automatic counts).

Shingo says that pokayoke should be thought of as having both a short action cycle (where immediate shut down or warning is given), and also a long action cycle where the reasons for the defect occurring in the first place are investigated. John Grout makes the useful point that one drawback of pokayoke devices is that potentially valuable information about process variance may be lost, thereby inhibiting improvement.

Richard Chase has extended Shingo's work to Services. He discusses stages of failsafing by both the provider and the customer. The service provider's work should attempt to be failsafed at the task stage (doing the actual work), at the treatment stage (the interaction with the customer - for instance customer greeting), and with the tangibles (the physical appearance, cleanliness etc). On the Customer side, failsafing could be attempted at three stages, equivalent to Vandermerwe's Pre, During, and Post stages of customer service. (See page 99).

	Control	Warning
Contact	Parking height bars Armrests on seats	Staff mirrors Shop entrance bell
Fixed Value	French fry scoop Pre-dosed medication	Trays with indentations
Motion Step	Airline lavatory doors	Spellcheckers Beepers on ATMs

after: Richard Chase and Douglas Stewart, Mistake-Proofing: Designing Errors Out, Productivity, 1995

A systematic way to consider failsafing is to construct a Cycle of Service diagram (see separate section), and then for each Moment of Truth consider how it may be failsafed.

Source inspection is simply the concept of responsibility for quality at the point of value adding. As a manufactured product progresses defects become more and more imbedded and so more costly to rectify. Hence the sensible thing is for the human operator to do self inspection, or at worst inspect the previous process. So source inspection is about moving away from dedicated inspectors and towards point of action inspection. The prime rule is "never knowingly pass on a defective". Note that this happens in service also - a typist should self check a letter before handing it on for signature.

Further reading
Shigeo Shingo, *Zero Quality Control : Source Inspection and the Pokayoke System,* Productivity Press, 1986
Richard Chase and Douglas Stewart, "Make Your Service Fail Safe", *Sloan Management Review*, Spring 1994, pages 35-44
Hroyuki Hirano, *Poka-Yoke: Improving Product Quality by Preventing Defects*, Productivity Press, 1989
Web site on Shingo
The Shingo prize for Lean and Quality. Details at http://www.shingoprize.org
An impressive site with numerous examples and pictures is at: http://campbell.berry.edu/faculty/jgrout/pokayoke

Taguchi

Genichi Taguchi is a Japanese statistician and engineer whose concepts only began to make an impact in the West during the 1980s. His principal contributions have been to our understanding of what product specification really means for quality and how such specifications can be translated into cost effective production. Quality through design could be a short summary.

Taguchi has been critical of the conventional view of quality acceptance, which is that there are specification limits within which a product is acceptable and beyond which it not. This black-and-white or perfect and defective is not the way most customers see quality, nor is it effective in a design or engineering sense, argues Taguchi. For instance, a meal served in a restaurant is not suddenly defective on one side of a particular temperature and perfect on the other. Nor would part dimensions which when changed by a fraction of a millimetre suddenly become defective. Taguchi argues instead for a continuous decline in utility as one moves further away from the target or optimal value. Taguchi refers to this as the "loss function". The function is called this because, Taguchi maintains, any deviation involves a "loss to society" over the lifetime of the product. He maintains that the loss is approximately proportional to the square of the deviation from the target value. That is, as the distance away from the target value doubles, the "loss" will increase by four times. Another interesting view is that there are "customer tolerance limits" rather than engineering or designer specified limits. So although there may be no sharp cutoff of acceptability as far as the design specification is concerned, there will eventually be limits beyond which a customer finds the product or service unacceptable.

Acceptance of the loss function has an important implication for quality improvement. Instead of crossing the limit to achieve acceptance and then ceasing further improvement effort, the loss function would suggest that improvement must be ongoing until the target perfection is achieved. Specification limits become superfluous. This ultimate goal is virtually impossible (there will always be a new magnitude of accuracy to challenge) so the improvement effort must never cease. Perhaps this would explain the apparent Japanese devotion to improvement (in Japan the Taguchi view is more well established) in contrast to more relaxed behaviour elsewhere.

Taguchi believes that it is preferable to design a product which is robust or insensitive to variation in the manufacturing process than it is to attempt to control all the many variations during actual manufacture. Instead of taking measures to control factors which degrade the performance of a product ("noise"), he believes in reducing their influence. Taguchi is fond of quoting an example from tile making where, instead of trying to control all the factors, such as temperature and pressure, and human error, which have an influence on tile dimensions, by altering the tile mix the process becomes much more robust to changes in these factors.

Some TAGUCHI concepts

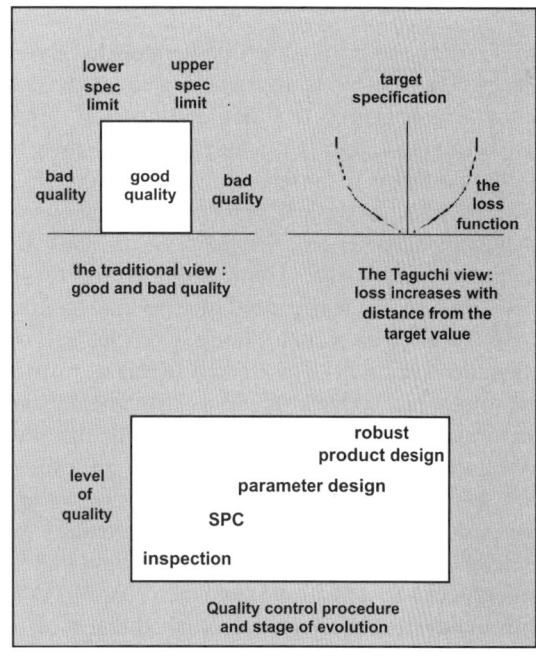

Like many great ideas, this is beautifully obvious. The trick is to put it into practice. This is where Taguchi's ideas on parameter design and the control of experiments come in. Experimental design is a well established body of knowledge in the field of statistics and was not invented by Taguchi. But Taguchi has made these concepts more usable and practical for the quality professional. In traditional statistical analysis, often scores of experiments have to be carried out to identify the sensitive parameters. This often puts their practical use out of bounds, but with Taguchi's methods the amount of work is drastically reduced. The object of the experiments is to identify the design parameter settings that minimise the effect of "noise", by systematically varying the design parameters and the noise factors and observing the outcome. Whilst it is true that Taguchi methods are probably beyond the statistical abilities of most operators, they can be appreciated by managers and used by designers. With the Taguchi view, design is the principal determinant to the final product cost, over its lifetime. A distinction is therefore made between "off line" quality control, which includes sensitivity tests and reliability tests, and "on line" quality control which is concerned with control during manufacture.

As Taguchi sees it, product development has three stages. The first, "system design", is a non statistical stage which brings together engineering and marketing/customer knowledge to produce a prototype design. In the second, "parameter design", the relationship of desirable product performance to changing parameters is explored. This amounts to finding a robust design, in other words the most cost effective way in which performance can remain good irrespective (within limits) of changes in operating conditions. The "secret" of this is to use the non-linear effects of product parameters on performance characteristics. (Refer to the tile example). The third stage is "tolerance design" which now sets tolerances around the target settings, not by the usual engineering techniques relating to "tolerance stackup", but by finding the right trade-off between society loss and manufacturing cost. All this sounds terribly complex. It is not, but it is also not simple. There are now thousands of successful examples.

We can view Taguchi methods along a continuum, being that inspecting the process (SPC) is superior to inspecting the product (SQC). And reducing the sensitivity of parameters is an advance on SPC because the process does not have to be so tightly controlled. And best of all is robust design where product performance remains good in spite of changes in operating characteristics.

Further reading
Genichi Taguchi, *System of Experimental Design*, UNIPUB Kraus, 1985

Glen Stuart Peace, *Taguchi Methods : A Hands-On Approach*, Addison Wesley, 1993

Kano

Dr. Noriaki Kano is a Japanese academic who is best known for his excellent "Kano model". The Kano Model has emerged as one the most useful and powerful aids to product and service design and improvement available.

The Kano model relates three factors (which Kano argues are present in every product or service) to their degree of implementation or level of implementation, as shown in the diagram. Kano's three factors are Basic (or "must be") factors, Performance (or "more is better") factors, and Delighter (or "excitement") factors. The degree of customer satisfaction ranges from "disgust", through neutrality, to "delight".

A Basic factor is something that a customer simply expects to be there. If it is not present the customer will be dissatisfied or disgusted, but if it is fully implemented or present it will merely result in a feeling of neutrality. Examples are clean sheets in a hotel, a station tuner on a radio, or windscreen washers on a car. Notice that there may be degrees of implementation: sheets may be clean but blemished. Basic factors should not be taken for granted, or regarded as easy to satisfy; some may even be exceptionally difficult to identify. One example is course handouts which a lecturer may regard as trivial but the audience may regard as a basic necessity. If you don't get the basics right, all else may fail - in this respect it is like Maslow's Hierarchy of Needs : it is no good thinking about self esteem needs unless survival needs are catered for. Market surveys are of limited value for basics (because they are simply expected). Therefore a designer needs to build up a list by experience, observation and organised feedback.

A Performance factor can cause disgust at one extreme, but if fully implemented can result in delight. This factor is also termed "more is better" but could also be "faster is better" or "easier is better". Performance factors are usually in existence already, but are neutral, causing neither disgust nor delight. It is not so much the fact that the feature exists, it is how it can be improved. The challenge is to identify them, and to change their performance. Examples are speed of check in at a hotel, ease of tuning on a radio, or fuel consumption. Performance factors represent real opportunity to designers and to R&D staff. They may be identified through market surveys, but observation is also important, especially in identifying performance features that are causing dissatisfaction. Creativity or process redesign is often required to deliver the factor faster or more easily, and information support may play a role as in the "one minute" check-in at some top hotels. The Cycle of Service (see separate section) is a useful starting point to identify performance factors.

THE KANO MODEL

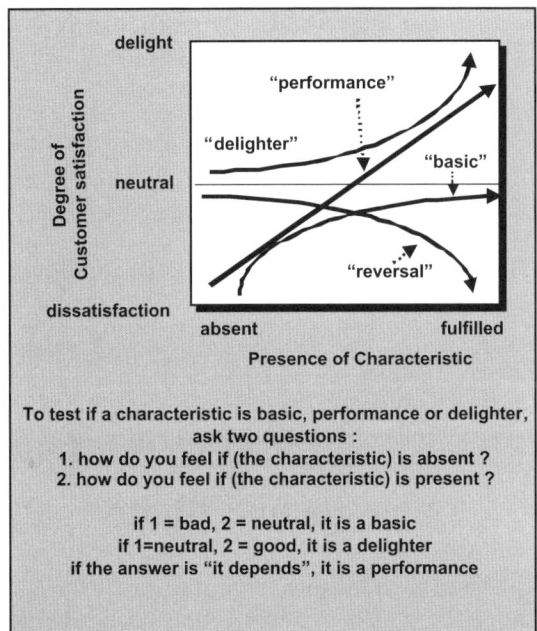

Finally, A Delighter is something that customers do not expect, but if present may cause increasing delight. Examples are flowers and wine awaiting guest arrivals in some hotel rooms, or a radio tuner that retunes itself when moving out of range of a transmitter. By definition, market surveys are of little use here. Once again, it is creativity, based on an appreciation of (latent) customer needs that can provide the breakthrough. But we need to be careful about Delighters also : a true Delighter is provided at minimal extra cost - it would certainly cause customer delight to give them all a complimentary car, but would be disastrous for company finances. Therefore, perhaps a more appropriate hotel Delighter would be to give guests a choice of sheet colour, pillow type (English or German), and sheet type (linen, satin, or cotton).

We should also note that the Kano factors are not static. What may be a Delighter this year may migrate towards being a Basic in a few years time. And also, what may be a Delighter in one part of the world may be a Basic in another. Thus it is crucial to keep up to date with changing customer expectations. Benchmarking may be a way to go. From Kano we also learn that a reactive quality policy, reacting to complaints, or dissatisfiers, will at best lead to neutrality but proactive action is required to create delight.

The Kano Model works well with Quality Function Deployment. Basics should be satisfied, and delighters can be explicitly traded off in the "roof" of the QFD matrix (for example fuel consumption may suggest a lighter car, but safety suggests a stronger one - so the quest is to find material that is light, strong, and inexpensive.)

Further reading:
Special Issue on Kano's Methods: *Center for Quality of Management Journal,* Vol 2, No 4, Fall 1993 (Several artices, including administering Kano questionnaires).

Hofmeister, Walters, Gongos, "Discovering Customer WOW's", *Annual Quality Congress*, ASQC, May 1996, pp759-770.

Joiner, B.L., *Fourth Generation Management*, McGraw Hill, New York, 1994

Lou Cohen, *Quality Function Deployment*, Addison Wesley, Reading MA, 1995, pp 36-41

Christian Grönroos and the Finnish School

Christian Grönroos is Professor of Service and Relationship Marketing at the Hanken Swedish School of Economics and Business, Finland. Grönroos is considered a Guru of service quality not only for his own contributions but because he has been a stimulant for much innovative thinking in the service area. The following are a few of the excellent contributions made by Grönroos and his associates.

Service Dimensions

Like Garvin's dimensions of product quality and Zeithaml's SERVQUAL dimensions for service (see separate sections) Grönroos has produced a list of the "seven criteria of good perceived service quality". These are Professionalism, Attitudes, Trustworthiness, Servicescape, Credibility, Accessibility, and Recovery. (The acronym is PATS CAR). "Servicescape" is a phrase from Mary Bitner relating to the physical environment. An excellent checklist, perhaps more meaningful than Zeithaml's RATER dimensions.

A Framework for Service Quality Relationships.

Grönroos' Finnish associate Holmlund perceives service interactions taking place in a hierarchy of acts, episodes, sequences, and relationships. An act is the smallest transaction between a provider and a customer. Examples include handing over cash to be deposited at a bank and greeting a guest at a hotel (basically, a "moment of truth"). A series of acts constitute an episode: the entire visit to the bank; a full meal at the hotel. Over time episodes repeat to form a sequence: several visits to the bank; a complete stay at the hotel. Sequences may build into relationships. Ongoing relationship with the bank; repeat visits to a hotel. The customer's perception of the quality of an act builds expectations of episodes and sequences. Experience of relationships and sequences feeds back to expectations of episodes. This model helps understanding of the way in which customer relationships are formed, and aids understanding of the dynamics of service quality.

Expectations.

Quality is closely linked to expectations. Grönroos' group has usefully distinguished three types of expectation. *Explicit:* These expectations can be articulated by customers, but may be realistic or unrealistic. A management task is to help customers adjust unrealistic to realistic. *Fuzzy:* where customers are not able to define or formulate clear expectations but which nevertheless impact satisfaction. What do you expect from a theme park visit? Answer: Don't know, but quite a bit. Management has a role to translate these fuzzy expectations into explicit expectations. *Implicit:* These expectations are taken for granted. It is management's task to build understanding, because these factors are easily overlooked. What is an obvious need to a customer may simply not be recognised by the service provider.

Note the overlap with the Kano model. Implicits are Basics. Explicit may be Performance factors. Fuzzy and unrealistic factors, if managed correctly, have the potential to be Delighters. Like Kano, the model is dynamic. Fuzzy becomes explicit. Unrealistic may become realistic.

Further reading
Christian Grönroos, *Service Management and Marketing*, Second edition, Wiley, Chichester, 2000

Shainin and Bhote

The late Dorian Shainin, who died in 2000, is a "forgotten" guru of Quality probably because he did not seek publicity but worked as a consultant for a large number of companies many of whom were unwilling to share his remarkable methods. "Shainin Methods" are a powerful family of analytical and statistical tools which help identify what he termed the "Red X" (the root problem or dominant cause) as opposed to the "Green Y" (the field or total problem) and the "Pink X" (the second most important cause). Shainin extended design of experiments (DOE), and suggested improvements in SPC. His methods are a considerable advance on the "7 Tools" of Quality but require more advanced understanding. (Bhote is dismissive of the "7 Tools" calling them Kindergarden Methods). Shainin methods have wide application in manufacturing and service.

Keki Bhote worked for Motorola and using Shainin methods helped that company win the Baldridge award and to establish the Six Sigma methodology. Later, working as a consultant, he has done much to popularise Shainin methods. His books *World Class Quality* (first and second editions) describe Shainin methods in detail.

The Shainin / Bhote tools form a powerful set leading from problem identification through implementation and onto control. In other words PDCA, but far more specific than PDCA. Bhote divides the family of tools into four sections: Defining and measuring, Clue generation, DOE, and Transition to SPC. Many of the individual tools are briefly described in this book. Here we attempt an overall summary.

Defining and Measuring: This comprises a set of questions aimed at clarifying the problem area and making subsequent analysis more effective. For instance Bhote suggests looking at the history, at quantification, at which stage the problem is detected (can this be done earlier?), and at clarifying whether the problem is a reliability problem or a quality problem. Measurement requires examination – is the measurement system itself capable?

Clue Generation: The idea of this stage is to reduce a large number of possible causes to a much smaller number. The Multi-vari chart is a prime tool. The Concentration chart is a form of measles chart. Components Search is an efficient procedure used in assembly operations and involving disassembly and reassembly in different configurations. It helps to home in on which assembly step is possibly the "Red X". Paired Comparisons has wide application in service and manufacture and involves looking at successive pairs of items, one good and one bad, and noting the differences until a trend emerges. A more involved method is called the Tukey Test that is used where there is a parameter, say a dimension, that is thought to have an influence in whether the item is good or bad. When ranked by the parameter, if it turns out that performance is good, good, good, bad, bad, bad this is more significant than if good, good, bad, good, bad, bad. The Product Process Search is a related technique used where it is unclear if variation is as a result of the product (material) or the process. Here, identify the potential process variables. Take samples, measuring each variable, until eight good and eight bad are accumulated. This is usually sufficient data to home in on the Red X, using the earlier and later techniques.

DOE Stage. Following the short list of candidate causes, this stage homes in on the Red X. A Variables Search is used where there are 5 to 20 variables. It is described as similar to the algorithm for finding any number between 1 and 1000 by halving and asking which half over and over again. Full Factorial is used for 4 or less variables and involves the orthogonal array procedure described in a separate section. (Taguchi orthogonal arrays have been criticised by Bhote on clue identification, validity, cost, and effectiveness grounds). Thereafter comes "B vs. C" or better v. current to ensure that the chosen solution is truly better. This is done by alternating between the proposed and current methods, thereby ensuring that the "Hawthorne effect" (where the productivity gains were more to do with the effect of being observed than the variables themselves) does not happen.

Transition to SPC. The final stage is concerned with "holding the gains" through "Positrol" (an extended form of standardisation more or less using the six honest serving men – see separate section), and "Pre Control" (see separate section).

All in all, a hugely powerful methodology.

Further reading
Keki Bhote and Adi Bhote, *World Class Quality*, (Second Edition), AmaCom, New York, 2000

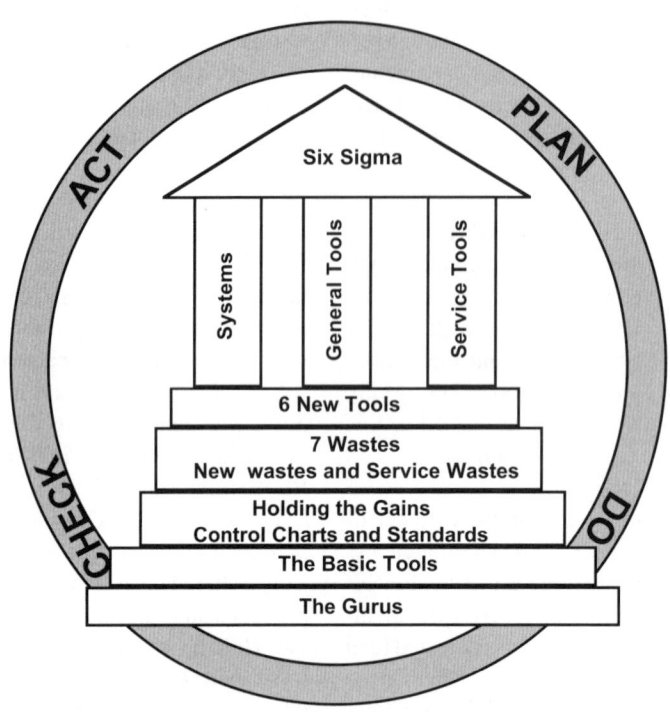

Improvement Cycles

PDCA and DMAIC

PDCA and DMAIC

The Deming Cycle is a universal improvement methodology. The original is PDCA (Plan, Do Check, Act) but there are many variations some with catchy acronyms like DRIVE (Define, Review, Investigate, Verify, Execute). Here we will discuss the original and the Six Sigma (DMAIC) versions. PDCA is the underlying concept of very many concepts in this book, and the foreword contains a table with the PDCA and DMAIC stages and how they relate to the tools in the book.

PDCA and SDCA

Deming originally called the PDCA cycle "the Shewart Cycle" after his mentor and father of statistical quality control, but the cycle has come to be named after Deming himself. PDCA sounds simple and is easily glossed over, but if well done is a powerhouse for improvement. PDCA is considered a foundation of the Toyota Production System. In the West many organisations are apt to just "do" and neglect the P-C-A. Incidentally, Kurt Lewin's ideas on Force Field Analysis (see separate section) and "unfreezing, changing, refreezing" is a variation of PDCA.

Plan. Plan is not just about planning what to do, but about communication, "scoping", discussion, consensus gaining and deployment. Begin with the customer - seek to understand their requirements. It is about setting the time plan. It is claimed that leading Japanese companies take much longer to plan, but then implement far faster and more smoothly. Deming taught that one should think about change and improvement like a scientific experiment – predicting, setting up a hypothesis, observing, and explaining deviations. You need to be clear what the goals are, and how to get there. Attempt to identify constraints beforehand, so force field analysis is a good idea. Try to identify root causes - at least ask the 5 whys. You may have to do some training before proceeding.

Do. An easy stage if you have planned well. It is about carrying out the improvement, often in a test phase.

Check. The learning stage, but too frequently an opportunity lost. Is it working as you predicted? Did it work out as planned? If not, why not, and what can we learn for next time? The US Marines call this "after action review" or AAR. Time needs to be set aside to Check. Like at the end of a meeting, or after completion of a set number of cycles. Keki Bhote refers to B vs. C (Better vs. Current) analysis. This is to see if the improvement is sustained or as a result of the "Hawthorne effect' which ceases when observation ceases. Six Sigma black belts would check the statistical significance – assessing the alpha and beta risks (accepting what should have been rejected, and vice versa). Once again ask about root causes. Also check if there are any outstanding issues.

PDCA

Plan	Determine customer needs Identify the concern or problem Set objectives Set out the working plan Collect data and study Seek root causes Train as necessary
Do	Implement the improvement

Check	Were the objectives met?
	Review root causes
	Confirm the results "B vs C" analysis
	(consider alpha and beta risks)
	After Action Review
	    what was learned?
	    what can be done better next time?
	Is the problem completely solved?

Act	Identify further improvements Write and adopt new standards Communicate the requirements Recurrence prevention Celebrate and congratulate

Act (or Standardise). As Juran says, "Hold the gains". A standard reflects the current best and safest known way, but is not fixed in stone forever. Without this step all previous steps are wasted. So, a vital, but frequently neglected, step. Think about improvement as moving from standard to improved standard. A deviation from standard procedures indicates that something is amiss. (See the section on standardisation). Consider if the new way can be incorporated elsewhere. Communicate the requirements to everyone concerned - this includes people on the boundary of the problem. Give some thought to recurrence prevention - can both the people and the processes be made more capable? Finally prepare for the next round of the cycle by identifying any necessary further improvements. And don't forget to celebrate and congratulate if gains have been achieved.

The SDCA or standardise, do, check, act emphasises stability. If variability is excessive it is difficult to distinguish between real improvement and chance variation. In this case, stabilise first before planning. (But see also Special and Common causes).

At AQC in 2001, Monte Lee Matthews suggested that an improved loop should be Plan Do Knowledge Act. That is, make a specific attempt to gain knowledge or lean. Matthews referred to Deming who said that theory was the basis of all knowledge. So have a theory, and check it to gain knowledge as part of the PDCA loop. It's the scientific approach.

A last word: Don't let the Deming PDCA cycle stand for "Please Don't Change Anything".

DMAIC

The Six Sigma methodology uses a variation of PDCA known as DMAIC (or Define Measure Analyse Improve Control). This has added several useful points. (See also the section on Six Sigma). You will notice that there is not a one-to-one relationship between PDCA and DMAIC. DMAIC has expanded upon the critical "Plan" stage.

Define. Define the problem.
Substages are identify opportunities and scope the project.
Choosing the right project also means not doing an alternative project. An organisation or improvement team has limited time so should select carefully. Use Pareto. Use Cost of Quality analysis. Begin with customer priorities. Be specific on project aims; go SMART (simple, measurable, agreed-to, realistic, and time-based). Six Sigma is strong on financial returns, so a savings estimate should be made. Scoping the project is critical - where are the problem boundaries, and what will be considered outside and inside? Of course, the "project" will be found within a process, not necessarily a department. So, "systems thinking" is required. "Seek not to be reductionist" to quote Systems Guru Peter Checkland.

Measure. How are we doing?
The substages are: analyse the problem process and define the target outcomes.
Six Sigma places strong emphasis on measurement. Find a suitable measure – preferably related to the process customer or output. Six Sigma prefers to use quantitative rather than qualitative data. Think defects per million opportunities. Are current measures appropriate? Define the measure clearly, the sources of the data, the sampling plan. Think validity (is what I am measuring a good indicator - preferably a lead indicator?)) and reliability (would another observer get the same result?). Think about appropriate defect classification – for instance record the total number of complaints in a hotel, or by type, by location, by customer? Check the consistency in the way defects are recorded. Also, be clear on the boundary of the process. See the section on defects per million opportunities (DPMO).

Analyse. What's wrong?
The substage is to do with getting onto root causes. Try to get to the root cause. Use the "7 tools" or process mapping. (See separate sections). The majority of tools in this book are useful here. Creative thinking, Benchmarking, QFD, Value Analysis, Design of Experiments, are but a few of the possibilities. Six Sigma places emphasis on statistical validation of results using tests.

Improve. Fix what is wrong.
Substages are prioritise and refine. See if you have got onto the real root cause.
Now you have to implement. "Go to Gemba" and do it. You may use Kaizen or Kaizen Blitz. You may also have to plan by using project management tools

Implementation should be preceded by Force Field Analysis done with the team.

Control. Hold the gains, and Sustain.
Verify. Measure again. And celebrate with the team. Set up SPC charts. Set new standard operating procedures. Test to see whether gains are real by going back to the old process and forward to the new.

Mikel Harry, one of the founders of Six Sigma, has extended the DMAIC cycle to Recognise, Define, Measure, Analyse, Improve, Control, Standardise, Integrate (*Quality Progress* - An Interview with Mikel Harry, Oct '99)

The Ford 8D Cycle is another improvement cycle possibility. The "8 D"'s are eight disciplines: (1) Use a team (2) Describe the problem (3) Contain the symptom (4) Find the root cause (5) Choose and verify the corrective action (6) Implement permanent corrective action (7) Prevent recurrence (8) Congratulate and celebrate.

Further reading.
Any book on Six Sigma.(Please refer to the Six Sigma section.)
Peter R Scholtes, *The Leader's Handbook: Making Things Happen Getting Things Done*. McGraw Hill, New York, 1999. Wirebound. Although not a book specifically on Six Sigma this is a great reference for many sections relating to the tools used with PDCA.

PDCA and DMAIC

Plan	Define	What is the problem?	Identify Opportunities Scope the Project
	Measure	How are we doing?	Analyse the Process Define Outcomes
	Analyse	What's wrong?	Identify Root Causes
Do	Improve	Fix what is wrong	Prioritise Refine Implement
Check Act	Control	Hold the gains. Celebrate.	Measure outcomes Acknowledge

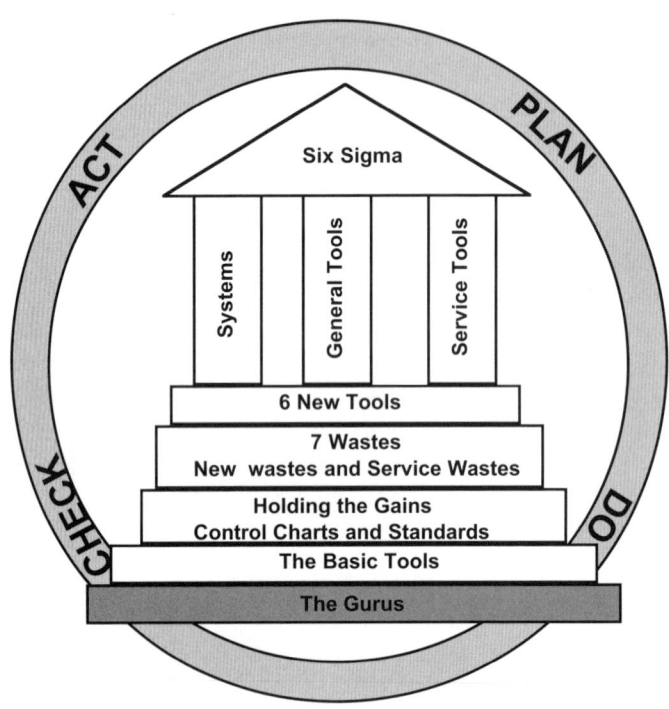

The 7 Tools

**Process Mapping
Pareto Analysis
Fishbone Chart
Histogram and Measles Chart
Run Diagram
Correlaton and Stratification
Check Sheets and Tally Charts**

(and Cross Impact Analysis)

The "7 Tools" of Quality

The seven tools of quality were originally assembled by Kaoru Ishikawa for use with quality circles. The seven tools, when used together or even individually, are a "first line" attacking force for quality improvement. They are taught to a large proportion of operators in Japan and are now increasingly used by operators worldwide. Many people in the service industry will find them equally useful. The tools are presented below in the order in which they are commonly used, although many variations are possible. Remember best used as a set in the order given below!

Mapping

There is a whole variety of mapping tools which are used in Process Reengineering, Lean Manufacturing, and Quality Management. Mapping tools often form a hierarchy. Thus, for instance, Seeing the Whole (Womack and Jones) may be used to map an entire value stream end-to-end across several companies, Value Stream Mapping (Rother and Shook) may be used to map a process wall to wall inside a plant, and process mapping may be used to home in the detail of a particular stage. There are mapping tools which are designed around service - The Cycle of Service, The Service Blueprint, and the Customer Processing Operation. These are described in the Service section of this book. Here we will concentrate on the process map, which forms one of the classic seven tools.

The Process Map

The process map lists every step that is involved in the manufacture of a product or the delivery of a service. It has long been used by work study officers, who usually use special symbols to indicate "operation", "delay", "move", "store", and "inspect". (See figure). The process chart helps identify waste, (or MUDA) and documents the process completely. Good communication is an important reason to do this. The systematic record helps reveal the possible sources of quality and productivity problems.

It is a good idea to draw the process map using the standard symbols because this aids clarity. The chart can be plotted against a time scale if time is critical. Process charts should also be used to document or standardise a process after it has been changed. This Standard Operating Procedure (SOP) can be used for "auditing" the process - to see if it is still being carried out in the way it was designed.

Many companies already have process charts. If they are available, beware! There are often differences between the "official" process charts and the way things actually happen in practice. The team or analyst should take the time to follow through a number of products. "Go to Gemba" (the place of action) and collect the facts; do not sit in the office and collect the opinions or the "normal" situation.

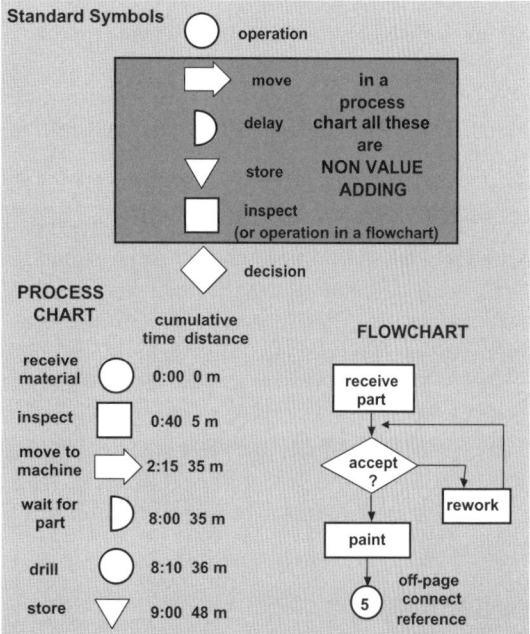

A flowchart is similar to a process chart and is often used when there are decisions involved. The symbol for a decision, a diamond, would lead to branching as a result of different decisions. Flowcharts are often used with computer systems and usually do not include the standard process chart symbols. However there is no reason why these symbols should not be combined.

Once the chart is assembled the individual activities

can be classified into those which add value (often a very small proportion), those which are pure waste and which should be eliminated as soon as possible, and those which are necessary non value added - necessary in the short term, but candidates for elimination in the long term.

In process reengineering it is common to draw maps left to right with rows to demarcate the organisational boundaries. Of course, a process map usually involves activities in several departments.

A process map is an activity and time based representation. Often it is useful to have a spacial diagram to hand as well. This "Spaghetti Diagram" maps the physical movement of operators.

All maps are best assembled using a team approach, preferably using the people who are "front line". By using the charts the team can begin systematically to document the nature of quality problems and defects. This leads onto the next tool.

Note : There is actually a family of process charts that is used by work study officers and industrial engineers. These are less frequently used by other staff, but they may be useful, particularly for productivity improvement. For instance, the "person-machine" process chart lists, against a time scale, what the person is doing side by side with what the machines that he/she is operating are doing. This enables wasteful time gaps to be identified. Details on these more specialized charts can be found in textbooks on Method Study.

Further reading
Dianne Galloway, *Mapping Work Processes*, ASQ Quality Press, Milwaukee, WI, 1994
Other Mapping Tools
Details of mapping tools more appropriate to plant-wide and supply chain mapping may be found in:
John Bicheno, *The Lean Toolbox*, PICSIE Books, Buckingham, 2000
Mike Rother and John Shook, *Learning to See*, Lean Enterprise Institute, Brookline, MA, 1998
See also sections on **Cycle of Service and Service Blueprinting**

Pareto Analysis.

Pareto analysis has been called "the single most powerful management technique of all time" (!). Alternative names are ABC analysis and the "80/20" rule. Pareto analysis gives recognition to the fact that, invariably, a small number of problem types account for a large percentage of the total number of problems that occur. The name "80/20" is representative of this; perhaps 80% of all problems are due to 20% of all the types of problem that occur. (Often 90/10 would be more typical.) The name ABC is also a good one. This suggests that the range of types of problem be classified into A, B, and C categories, designating their importance.

(Pareto analysis is also good practice in many other fields of management; for instance inventory control, forecasting, marketing, and personnel.)

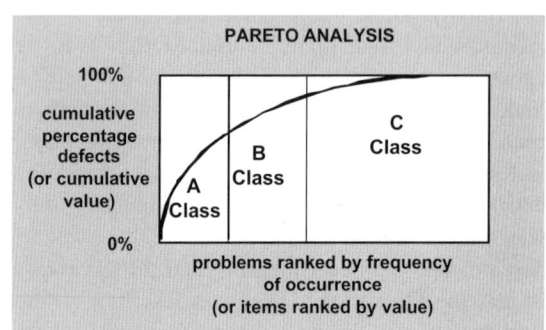

It makes good sense to tackle the most pressing problems first; the "vital few" as Juran calls them. When these are successfully eliminated or reduced, of course, another problem will head the list. So now tackle that one. And so on. Continuing in this way is an effective ongoing improvement methodology.

Pareto analysis begins by ranking problems from highest to lowest. See the example. Along the horizontal axis problems are arranged in order of frequency from highest to lowest. Then the cumulative number of problems is plotted on the vertical axis. It can be seen that the resulting graph rises rapidly then tails off to an almost flat plateau. Now it is easy to pick out how many problems need top priority attention.

Now the team has used the process chart to list and classify the problems, and Pareto analysis to identify the most serious problems. In the next stage the team would begin to explore possible causes and their solution.

The Fishbone Diagram

The Ishikawa diagram, also known as the "Cause and Effect" diagram and the "fishbone" diagram, is used to brainstorm out possible contributing causes of a particular problem or defect. In this respect it follows directly from the Pareto diagram, with the most pressing problem becoming the spine of the "fish". An example is shown in the figure. The name of "fishbone" is clearly representative of the form.

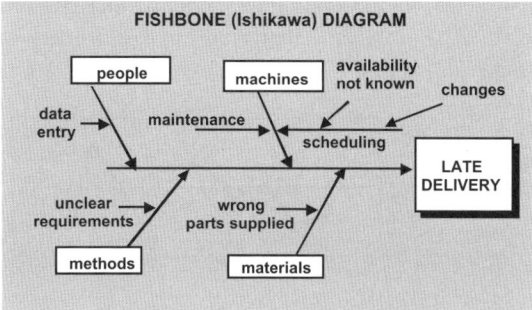

As can be seen, contributing causes are written in on the diagram, arranged in a hierarchy. Hence the name "cause and effect". If some difficulty is experienced in starting off the diagram, use the "6 M's" (men/people, machines, methods, materials, measures, mother nature) as initial "bones". Other alternatives for service operations are to use the "4 P's" (Places, Procedures, People, Policies), or the "4 S's" (Surroundings, Suppliers, Systems, Skills). Usually the diagram is built with one person writing in points on the diagram and a team contributing their ideas.

The beauty of the Ishikawa diagram is the concise and visual way in which contributing causes can be documented on one diagram. It requires literally seconds of instruction in order for any employee to understand.

A variation on the Ishikawa diagram is the "CEDAC" diagram, originally developed by Fakuda. CEDAC stands for "cause and effect diagram with addition of cards". It is the same Ishikawa diagram except that cards, containing notes and ideas on each particular cause, are added to the diagram. Usually there are slots made for each cause, giving access to a pocket into which cards are placed. This addition is very useful because it allows elaboration on the thinking. The diagram can be kept on display, and as further information or thoughts are acquired, they are added to the pockets. This prevents "reinventing the wheel". Fakuda has developed the CEDAC concept into a complete improvement methodology.

Now with the range of possible causes identified, it seems a good idea to firm up on the information that is available. This is where the next tool comes in.

Further reading
Ryuji Fakuda, *Managerial Engineering*, Productivity Press, 1983

The Histogram and Measles Chart

The histogram has much in common with the Pareto diagram. It is used to show graphically the relative number of occurrences of a range of events. Using vertical bars, it plots frequency on the vertical axis against events, arranged one after the other on the horizontal axis. (See the figure.)

Following from the Ishikawa diagram, data is collected and classified according to each of the causes suggested. This data is shown on a histogram, from which the most important causes should be apparent. As with the Pareto diagram, it is then clear which are the causes that require further investigation.

Histograms can be used to collect data literally as it happens. Here a flip chart is set up right at the workstation. As problems occur they are written down on the flipchart. When the same problem recurs, a tick is placed next to that problem. In effect this is building up a histogram. (In this case the histogram is lying on its side, but no matter.) The problems with the most ticks are obviously the most frequently occurring and most urgent problems. Such a "flipchart histogram" has the great advantages of being easy to use, visible for all, and up to date.

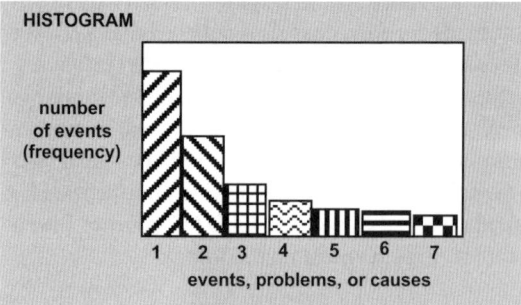

A special form of histogram, with similarities to the flip chart procedure, is the Measles or Concentration chart. Here defects or problems are simply plotted on an engineering drawing, blueprint or map at the location where the problem occurs. The accumulation of marks on the drawing gives an excellent impression as to where the problems lie. It avoids numerical or written description and may lead to the rapid identification of related problems. (A symmetry of the defects may indicate a process problem, but a lack of symmetry may indicate a maintenance or wear problem.) Of course, there are extensions of this technique - times can be written in, or different symbols used for different operators. Measles charts are also used for accident "black spots", and at Ford to indicate which areas are generating the most ideas for improvement. Juran tells the story of how such charts were used to assess damage on WWII bombers raiding Germany. Damage holes were uniformly spread except in some areas. Why? Because hits in those areas proved fatal. This lead to extra armour in those areas, resulting in a reduction in bombers shot down.

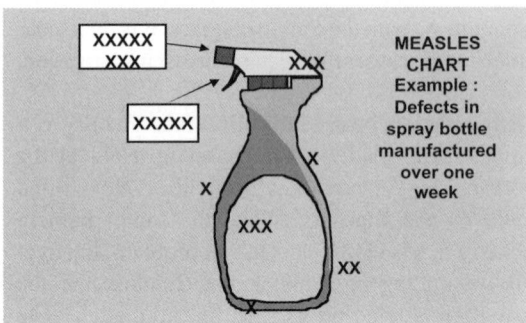

Run and Multi-vari Diagrams

Run diagrams and correlation diagrams are used to explore relationships between events and time, and between problems and possible causes,

The run diagram is simply a graph of the number of events plotted against time. It is truly amazing how many organisations ignore this simple but hugely effective tool. For instance, a record can be kept of the number of complaints over time. This may reveal that complaints occur at the beginning of the month or at a certain time of day. If defects produced on a machine are plotted against time, one may discover that most defects tend to occur when the machine has been used for some time (hot?) or just after the tea-break (carelessness?). A common use for a run chart is to detect slow trends (i.e. a gradual increase or decrease). For this, the charts have to be maintained over a long period.

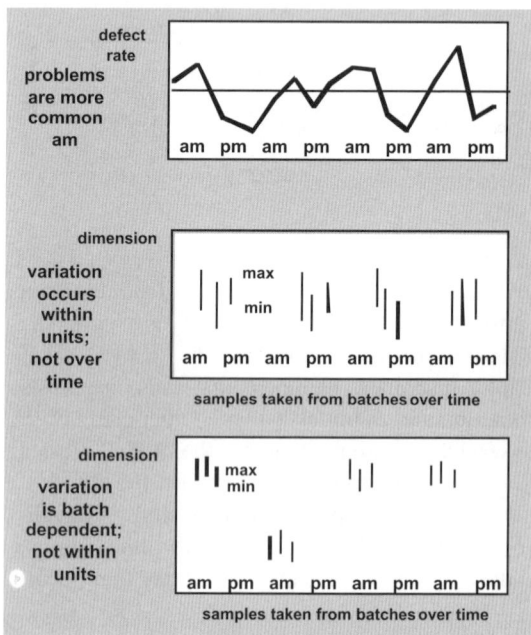

Multi-vari charts extends the run diagram concept to look at variation (a) by time - perhaps by hour, shift, day, week (b) by unit - variation within the same batch or time period and (c) within unit - say operator to operator, machine to machine, or across components within a product

Correlation and Stratification

The correlation diagram is used for more specific experimentation. Usually defect level (or some other measure of performance) is plotted on the vertical axis and the "experimental variable" on the horizontal. An example would be rejects against temperature. (Perhaps as temperature rises rejects fall, but then around a specific temperature rejects begin to increase again.) This could either be found out by a specific experiment involving deliberately varying the temperature, or by simply counting rejects and taking the temperature from time to time in the normal course of operation.

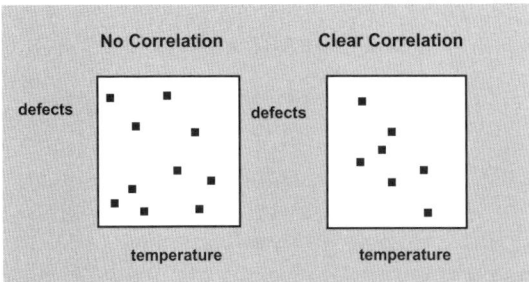

Very often no relationship (or "correlation") is found. So something else has to be tried. Perhaps first temperature, then pressure, then temperature divided by pressure, and so on. (In services, perhaps customer wait time against number of servers, or customer response time against quantity of information displayed on a screen.) Eventually, and with intelligent guesswork, good relationships can be found. This detective work can be a lot of fun, and front line people are often good at it because they have an appreciation of the real factors that make a difference. Normally an attempt is made to hold other factors as constant as possible while one factor at a time is varied.

There is a measure of correlation, called the "correlation coefficient", which can be calculated by formula. This measure is to be found "built in" on many scientific calculators, but is not given here. The reason why it is not given is that it is always preferable to plot the results on graph paper and to judge the relationship visually.

Often both run diagrams and correlation diagrams will be used. First a run diagram is used for more general analysis and to see if time of day or month has an effect. Then follows a correlation study for the specifics. There are other possibilities as well. A common one is the Tally Chart, where, for example, errors are recorded in a matrix which shows operator names along one axis and types of error or time of day along the other axis. This would reveal, perhaps, that different operators are good at different things or have different error-prone periods.

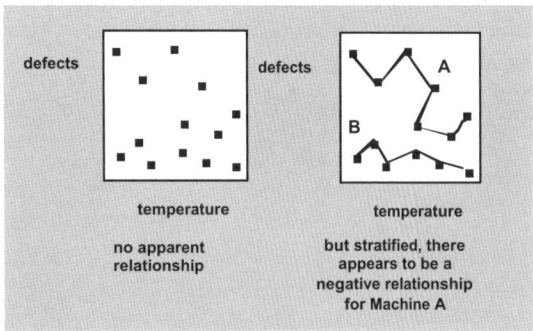

Stratification simply means splitting the data into groups and plotting the results on graphs. For instance, defect data against time may appear to have no particular pattern, but when data for individual operators or machines is plotted the situation may suddenly clarify. Clearly there is often a large number of ways in which data can be separated out; by operator, machine, material, time, batch, product, customer, location are just a few. But once a team knows about stratification they are likely to make good suggestions as to how it can be separated. Of course, this means that care has to be taken in the first place as to how the data is collected. It is a learning process.

Run diagrams, correlation diagrams and stratification have the effect of identifying what are termed "special causes". These are the events or defects which cannot be explained by natural variation of the process. (More on this later.) So having identified and solved some of these problems, it may now be time to set up a more sophisticated control mechanism to bring the process under control and to keep it under control.

Check Sheets and Tally Charts

There are several forms. "Aircraft style" checks would be carried out at the start of every shift or the start of each new batch, as an airline pilot would do before setting out. A process diagram, placed next to the machine or service counter, details what should be done and may advise what action to take in special circumstances.

Yet another variation is the Tally Chart. A typical variation is shown, but other variations include defect type against time, or defect against stage. The latter is sometimes referred to as a "Quality Filter Chart". Costs can also be added.

TALLY Chart

	Nick	Peter	John	Simon	Claire	
Burrs		𝍧 IIII	IIII		𝍧	14
Scratches	𝍧	𝍧 𝍧	III			18
Dents	IIII		II		II	8
Other		II			𝍧	7
	9	17	10	5	7	

QUALITY FILTER Chart

Stage	Defects / month	FTT %	Cost per month
Blank	32	98%	$ 68
Press	1624	88%	$ 2166
Assemble	533	58%	$ 9873
Paint	110	94%	$ 7985
Ship	12	99%	$ 564

Note: FTT = First Time Through

One special form of check sheet, used by Toyota, is related to the "Seven Wastes" and is a sheet containing perhaps 50 questions that ask operators if particular events are taking place. ("Do you have to reach to grasp a control?", "Do you have to take more than two paces to collect parts?".) These are further discussed under the Seven Wastes.

Some Quality Experts regard Standard Operating Procedures (SOPS) as check sheets. SOPS are a vital tool to "hold the gains", but they are not tools for analysis. For this reason they are dealt with in the next section.

Cost Impact Analysis:
A Good Tool to Use with All 7 Tools.

A simple but useful tool to use with all the tools is the Cost (or difficulty) Impact Analysis. The matrix is shown below. Its use is obvious. Go for the easy to do "the low hanging fruit" first. The matrix can also be used with any technique that generates several alternatives.

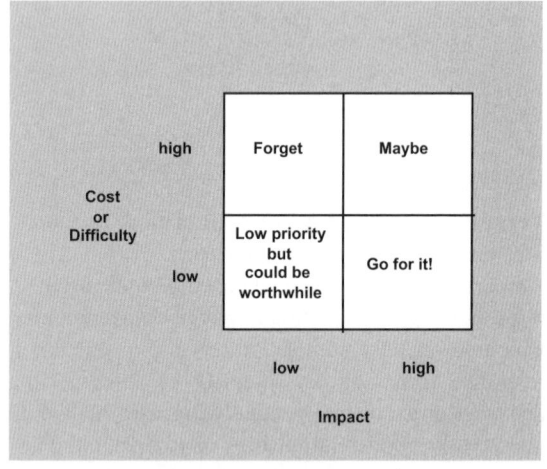

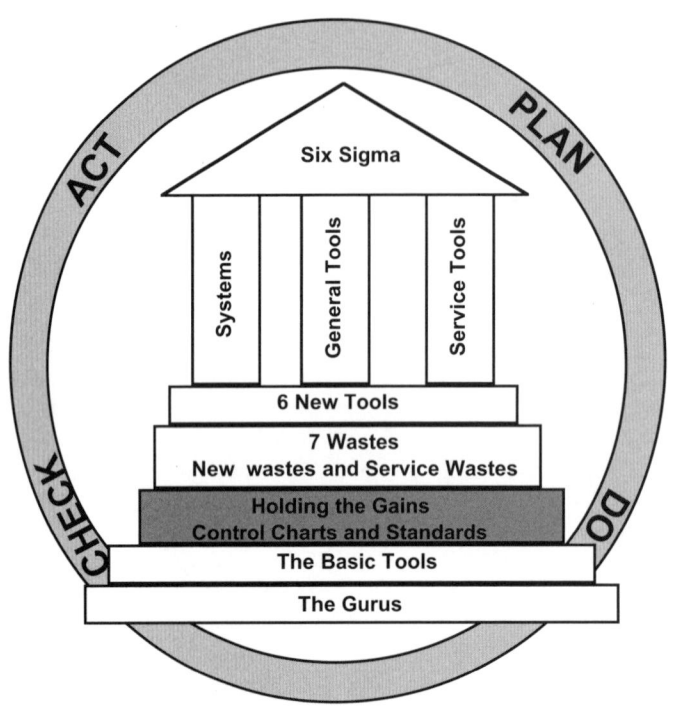

Holding the Gains

**Statistical Process Control (SPC)
Process Capability
Standards and Standard Operating Procedures**

Holding the Gains

The 7 Tools are the basics for the "Plan" stage of the PDCA cycle. Then comes implementation (Do) and Check. The last stage is to hold the gains and to standardise the new way. Without this stage all previous work may be lost. Two of the principal tools for this are described here:

Statistical Process Control (SPC)

Statistical process control (SPC) aims at achieving good quality during manufacture or service through prevention rather than detection. It is concerned with controlling the process (or machine) which makes the product. If the process is good, then the products will automatically be good. So the process or machine which makes the product is inspected rather than inspecting the product itself. This is really proactive management - inspecting and controlling the process before the event, rather than reactive management - inspecting the product after the event. SPC charts are like the temperature gauge in your car. Things are fine as long as temperature remains in the green zone, but if in the red zone you should stop and investigate.

SPC is not of course the full answer to total quality. A poorly designed product can conform to all manufacturing requirements, but still fail to convince customers that it is a quality product.

Perhaps confusingly at first, the best way to find out what is happening to a process is to take measurements of the products that the process is producing. Of course you do not need to look at every product that is produced. Instead you take samples, and use statistics to judge what is happening to the process. This is why it is called statistical process control. It may seem as if one is inspecting a few of the products coming out of the process, but in fact it is the process that is being inspected and controlled.

SPC is undertaken through the use of charts on which the performance of the process is plotted. If the process starts to go haywire it can be stopped in good time before many or any defectives are made.

Natural variation of the process

Every process has natural variation. (Refer also to the Deming section). In other words, it is impossible to make any product with absolute consistency. The inconsistency will be caused by chance variations, however small, in, perhaps, the material, tool wear, positioning of the piece, speed of the machine, actions by the operator, and so on. These are called common causes. This variation can be measured and, using statistics, its spread can be predicted. It turns out that the spread follows a particular pattern, known as the normal distribution, irrespective of the type of process, so long as samples are being taken, and there are not "special events" taking place. The special events are "assignable" to unusual or unexpected changes or events, which may cause defects to be produced.

99.7% of normal variation takes place within plus and minus three standard deviations (a standard deviation is a measure of spread, and every normal distribution has this characteristic.) The upper and lower control limits are set at plus and minus three standard deviations. Within this range we say that natural variation is occurring. However if an unusual event or "special cause" takes place, the reading or sample may fall outside of the control limits. Now we would need to stop and investigate. This is just like variation in the temperature gauge in your car. Natural variation occurs when going up a long hill or on a hot day or by hard driving. But the temperature remains in the normal range. If however the fan belt breaks or the coolant leaks, this would soon show up a temperature in the red zone, beyond the "control limit". You stop and investigate. If you do not you are foolish. Likewise you might undertake routine maintenance but it would also be foolish to overreact when the gauge is showing that temperature in within the acceptable zone. So it is important to know where the limits are located.

Types of chart : variables and attributes

There are two main types of chart - variables and attributes. A variables chart measures some characteristic that is variable along a scale, such as length or the number of scratches. It is something that can be measured. An attribute chart is used where the possibilities are pass or fail, yes or no. With an attribute, a judgement is made rather than a measurement taken.

Selecting the Right Control Chart

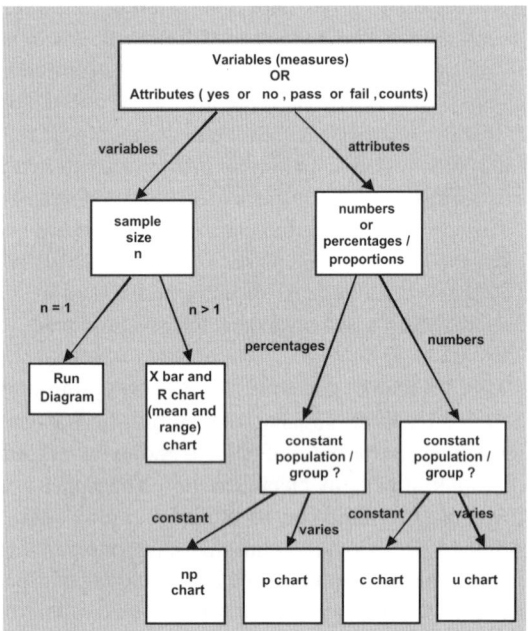

Variables charts : The average and range chart

The main variables chart is the "average and range" chart, also known as the "x bar and r chart". This is actually two charts, one which tracks the average measurement of the sample taken, and the other the range of the sample, that is the maximum minus the minimum value. Both are necessary. For instance the average of a sample of five may be fine, but the range could be unacceptably wide. And the range could be small, but located in the wrong place; that is it has an undesirable average. So typically, at random intervals throughout the day, the operator will take, say, the five most recent products produced and set them aside. This is a "sample". The particular product dimension is measured and the average and range values of the sample calculated. These two results are plotted on the chart, usually by the process operator. The chart indicates if the process is "in control". If it is, work continues. If not, work stops and investigation begins. Note that it is possible to be out of control and still not be producing defects, and vice versa.

Refer to the figure. Notice that both the average and the range charts have an upper and a lower "control limit". These limits are the bounds beyond which the process is considered "out of control". (See page 40).

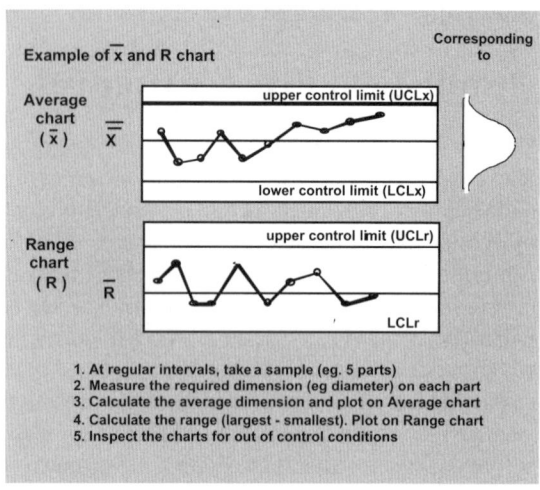

Setting up the control chart

Charts must be set up for each process - that is for each machine making a particular type of product. (Pre-printed SPC charts are available from some Quality societies or in books, and these make data entry and chart plotting very easy.) When setting up a chart it is important that there is consistency, so samples should be taken over a representative period of time. You will need to decide on a sample size and the number of samples. Typical numbers are a sample size of 5 and at least 20 samples. For each sample calculate the average ("mean") and the range. Refer to the figure. Then calculate the average of the averages, and the average of the ranges. Now you will need to look up the control limit factors for the sample size you have used. (If you have used a sample size of 5, the factors are given in the figure.) Now use the formulas in the figure to calculate the control limits. When these are drawn in you can begin to use the charts for control purposes. You will have to decide a reasonable average interval for samples to be taken. Generally, the higher the "Cpk" value, the less frequent does the sampling have to be. (See the section which follows on capability.)

Attribute charts : p, c and u charts

It is not always possible to measure variables. Some defects, such as scratches, tears, and holes are either there or they are not. The products either pass or they do not. This is where "p" (percentage) and "c" charts come in. p Charts are used where there are batches of product and the percentage that are defective can be determined.

With attributes there is only one chart that is plotted, not two as with the average and range chart. But the basic concepts of controlling variation, of taking samples, of setting up the charts, and of interpreting them remain. Only the formulas are different.

SPC FORMULAS

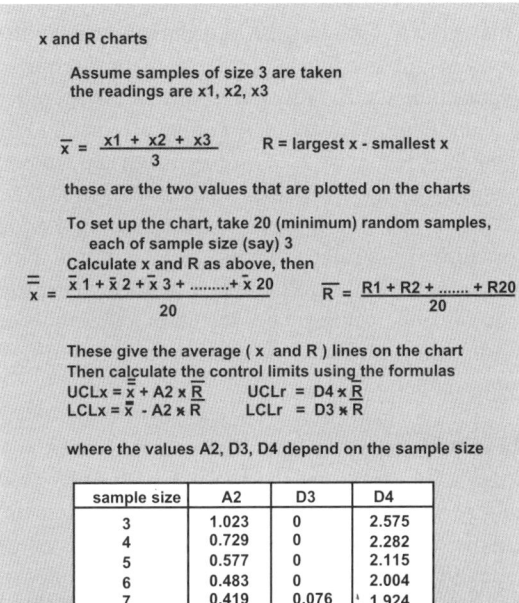

A "c" chart is used to monitor the number of nonconformities per product. Examples are the number of complaints per period, the number of scratches per table top, or the number of errors per processed document. In such cases a percentage figure is less meaningful, so a P chart cannot be used. "c" charts are particularly useful in service situations and are instantly usable because the formula is so easy to remember.

To use a c chart, the number of units sampled should be approximately the same. The control limits for a c chart are at :

$$c +/- 3\sqrt{c}$$

where c is the average value per sample. So if the average number of scratches per sample of 10 tables is 16, then the control limits are at $(16 + 3x4) = 28$ and $(16 - 12) = 4$. Therefore if 30 scratches are detected, the process is out of control. Such an easy to calculate control limit should be known to every service manager to monitor, for example, the number of complaints in a week or the number of nonconformities in a sample of 10 hotel room makeups or the number of late deliveries. Simply find the average number of complaints, take the square root of the average number, and add three times the square root to the average to give the control limit. A significant change has occurred if the number of complaints or nonconformities exceeds this control limit. The only condition to be aware of in using this fast check is that the "population" or units on which this data is gathered is approximately the same. For example, you can use the formula if the hotel occupancy is approximately constant, or the total number of deliveries is about the same. If not, use the following:

Where the number of units is not constant, simply replace "c" by "u" where $u = c/n$ and n is the number of units. The control limit formula is then

$$u +/- 3\sqrt{(u/n)}$$

Chart interpretation

There are other criteria, apart from falling outside of the control limits, that indicate an out of control situation. These other criteria can also be identified by operators, so that early action can be taken. With natural variation occurring you would expect measurements to be spread more or less evenly on either side of the average value. To be more precise, with the standard deviation known, you would expect a certain proportion of measurements to fall within plus and minus one, two, and three standard deviations of the average value. If this does not occur, again there is an indication of trouble. As an example, the probability of a measurement falling above the average is, of course, 50%. The probability of two successive measures above the mean is 25% (.5 x .5). And the probability of three successive measures above the mean is 12.5% (.5 x .5 x .5). Four successive above is 6.25%, and so on. If we get to seven successive measures above the average the probability is less than 1%, and we could reasonably conclude that something unusual (a special event) has taken place. Other out-of-control criteria are linked with the probabilities of successive measurements falling beyond a particular number of standard deviations. A full list can be found in texts on SPC.

The interpretation of control charts is a skill that can be developed. Particular chart patterns are indicative of particular problems that may be developing. Some indications are given in the figure.

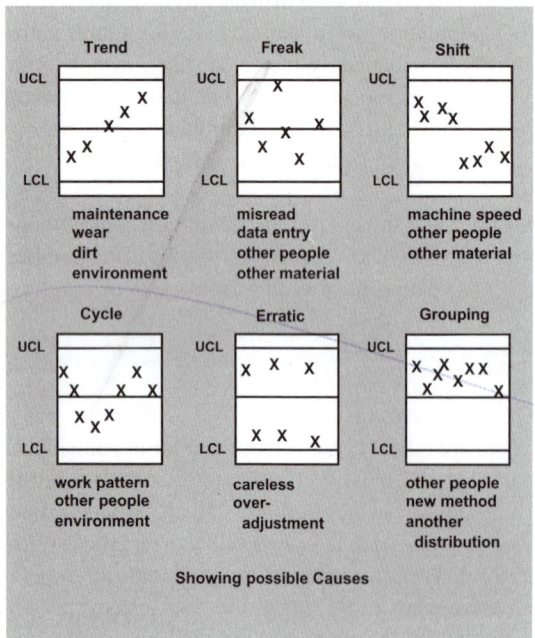

Common Causes and Special Causes

If variation takes place between the control limits we say that the process is in control and common causes are at work. It is stable. If an unusual event takes place (as a result of a change in people, materials, methods, machine, mother nature) the point would plot outside of the control limits and we would say the process is "out of control". Deming was famous for accusing managers of not understanding the difference between common cause and special cause variation. The former should be ignored, but definite action be taken in case of the latter. Of course, a stable process is not necessarily good. For instance, you can have a high level of complaints that nevertheless remain within the control limits. Such a process would be in control but not capable.

Process Capability

This section will largely be concerned with the capability of machines to operate within required tolerance limits. However, the concept of capability is wider than just machines. People also need to be capable. Whether we are concerned with machines or people John Oakland points out that we should not be asking, in the first instance, "are we doing the job correctly?", but rather "are we capable of doing the job correctly?". Capability refers to having the clear requirements, appropriate selection of people or machines, adequate training, and adequate measurement.

As noted above, being "in control" does not necessarily mean that the process is making good quality products. So there is another requirement. This is referred to as "process capability". Process capability refers to the match between the location of the upper and lower process control limits (UCL and LCL) and the specification limits USL and LSL (also known as tolerance limits UTL and LTL). The location of the process control limits is due to the natural variation of the process that makes the product. The specifications of the product, on the other hand, are given by the designer or manager of the product or service. These are two distinctly separate things, but they must relate in order to produce quality products.

It is important that process capability should not be measured before the process is "in control". In other words, if there are assignable causes and special events to be sorted out, this must be done first. These assignable causes are by their nature unpredictable, and have an unpredictable effect on the process control measures.

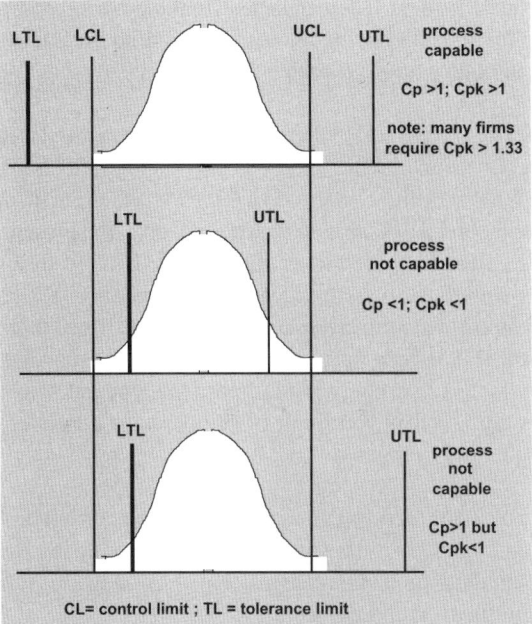

Process capability is measured by two ratios "Cp" and "Cpk". Cp is known as 'process potential' in Germany. The Cp measure simply compares the specification (or tolerance) spread with the process spread. Clearly if the natural spread of the process is wider than the spread of the specifications, (i.e. the Cp ratio is less than 1) then defectives are going to occur routinely. (Defectives will "seep out"; this is a way to remember the ratio names). But we need to also be concerned with where the process spread is located in relation to the specification limits. One could have a small process spread located outside of the specification limits. This would give a Cp value greater than 1 but would be unacceptable. So Cpk is needed.

Cpk is the smaller of two ratios :

(upper specification limit - process average value)
half the process spread

or

(process average value - lower specification limit)
half the process spread

Half the process spread is, of course, equal to the upper control limit minus the lower control limit. Refer to the diagrams. In practice, many companies insist on a Cpk value of at least 1.33 before the process is regarded as "capable". So "quality capable" means that the process or machine is both "in control" and has a Cpk value of at least 1.33. As the Cpk value goes above 1.33, the likelihood of defects declines so the need to take more frequent samples decreases. So it is always a good idea to seek to improve Cpk values even if the value of 1.33 has been reached. This can be done by many means including improved maintenance, better tool wear monitoring, closer working with suppliers, and improved training.

Six Sigma and Process Capability

The phrase "Six Sigma" refers to the specification limits being located at plus and minus six standard deviations. An aim of six sigma is therefore to drive down the spread of the natural variation of the process such that the distance from the mid point of the process spread to the nearest specification limit is six standard deviations. This would give a Cpk value of 2.0. Since the normal distribution (or the spread of the process variation) is theoretically infinite there is a small risk that defects will nevertheless be produced. This risk equates to .002 parts per million (ppm) or two parts per billion.

However, when Motorola was setting up the Six Sigma concept, they allowed for a process shift of plus or minus 1.5 standard deviations from the central point. This was apparently to account for the fact that real processes are not exactly centred or if centred tend to drift slightly. If a 1.5 standard deviation shift occurs there is of course an increased risk of producing defects. A 1.5 sigma shift would reduce the Cpk to 1.5. This works out at 3.4 parts per million (ppm) which is the famous six sigma target rate.

Some Problems with SPC

SPC is a powerful technique, but users must be aware of its limitations and assumptions.

Risk. Since we are dealing with statistical distributions there is a risk of saying it is out of control when it is not and saying a process is in control when it is not. These are known as alpha risk and beta risk respectively. These risks decrease with increasing capability. As noted, control limits are set up at plus and minus three standard deviations corresponding to 99.7% of the full distribution. So when the capability ratio is 1.0 the risk is 0.3% Likewise, a process with a capability ratio of 1.0 will be producing almost 3000 ppm.

Independence. One assumption is that of independent samples. By independent is meant there is no relationship one to another. But if, for instance, there is gradual tool wear then the samples may not be independent. Taking samples at regular intervals is not independent.

Ability to Detect Changes. As noted there are several tests for out of control conditions. One test is for seven successive points on the same side of the mean line. If samples are taken (say) on average once an hour, it may take 7 hours to detect an out of control condition.

SPC was in the news in 2000 when workers at BNFL failed to record the data conscientiously. Nothing was wrong with the process or the product, but the customer noticed some anomalies. The shipment of nuclear fuel had to be sent back, eventually costing the company millions of pounds and several senior managers their jobs. This case illustrates that SPC should never be regarded as mechanical and remote from the product. SPC should be about process improvement not just process monitoring.

Further reading
Charles Standard and Dale Davis, *Running Today's Factory*, Hanser Gardner, Cincinnatti, 1999.

Standards and Standard Operating Procedures

Standards are the basis for quality and continuous improvement. They make lean manufacturing possible. Standardisation allows you to "hold the gains", as Juran would say, rather than slip back to old ways.

To quote Henry Ford: "To standardize a method is to choose out of many methods the best one, and use it. What is the best way to do a thing? It is the sum of all the good ways we have discovered up to the present. It, therefore, becomes the standard. ... Today's standarization .. is the necessary foundation on which tomorrow's improvement will be based. If you think of 'standardization' as the best you know today, but which is to be improved tomorrow - you get somewhere. But if you think of standards as confining, then progress stops."

So a standard should simply reflect the current best and safest known way to do a task. Following the standard procedure means that it is easy to trace problems that may occur.

Toyota's Ohno realised that the achievement of standardised work, with minimum variance, was the essential ingredient to allow one piece flow and Lean production. Deming, in proposing the PDCA cycle, saw improvement moving from standard to standard. Juran emphasised the importance of "holding the gains" by establishing standards following a process improvement, rather than allowing them to drift back to the old ways. In service, McDonald's standard procedures fill a thick book. The company is known worldwide for the consistency of its products.

Recently the "Learning Organisation" has become fashionable, including "knowledge harvesting" from everyone in the organisation. How is this to be achieved? By documenting experience; in other words by establishing standards from which others may learn. Standards are the basis for training.

At Toyota, emphasis is placed on workers documenting their own standards, and in mastering both a wider range of work tasks and greater responsibility for supporting tasks. Operators themselves establish work cycles within the specified takt time. (Takt time is the smoothed rate of production, defined as actual work time divided by average number of products made.) It may be that they are assisted in this task by industrial engineers and supervisors, but the operators must write up the final documentation of work standards themselves. This achieves four goals. First, there can be no question that work standards are not understood. Second, the operator is forced to think about the best way in which he or she should do the work within the takt time. A trained operator will frequently do a better job than an uninvolved work study officer. Third, the responsibility for setting the standard and then maintaining it is clearly up to the operator. There is motivation to update the standard when improved ways are found. And, fourth, because the standards reflect what actually happens rather than what might happen, learning can take place rapidly when operators change jobs. In other words this is job enrichment and job mastery.

Too many operations-based organisations delude themselves on standards. It is tempting to simply impose work standards by getting industrial engineers or work study people to do the work and to post standards at workstations, or worse to keep them in a file. Then of course, there is no buy-in, no foundation for continuous improvement, and worst of all a great likelihood of large process variance. So the quick way turns out to be the least effective way and often a total waste. Traditional "Taylorism", is suitable only for the sweat shop. The Toyota way takes time to train operators to do the analysis and standardisation themselves - they need not only to learn basic work-study principles but also to appreciate the reasons why they should do it. Toyota regards work standardisation as one of its most challenging management tasks. Robert Hall believes that this worker-oriented standardisation, requiring high levels of operator skill and motivation is a key to the Toyota Production System.

So what should a standard contain? Operator standards should contain the essential work sequence steps that are involved together with the time taken for each step (these should be written in the operators own words), and the standard inventory quantity or kanban quantity involved during the takt time cycle. These should be supported by a diagram or photograph of key steps. Key process indicators, such as an hourly part count should be given. Particular points to look out for need to be given including notes on any special operation that is required to be carried out periodically. Standard procedures can be colour coded to match the product that carries a label of matching colour. When an engineering change occurs, the new product number should match the number on the new standard sheet. Often, a standard should cover not only what to do when things are normal, but also what to do if things go wrong. Consider health and safety. There should be "own responsibility" for the standard, for publishing it, for keeping it at the workplace, and for keeping it up to date.

At Intel where consistency is an absolute requirement, operators audit one another using the standard instructions. Toyata's designers accumulate check sheets reflecting lessons learned.

Managers and other workers should also consider documenting their standards. At least there should be broad standards for repetitive activities such as meetings, the budget cycle, personnel procedures, document preparation, placing of orders, appraisals, and so forth. The broad steps or a loose descriptive format may be appropriate. The same PDCA thoughts apply; if new form of meeting is found to work better than the old one, document both with comments on why the new way works better. But do it, otherwise the opportunity to learn may be lost.

Further reading
Robert W Hall, "Standard Work: Holding the Gains", *Target*, Fourth Quarter, 1998, pp 13-19
Henry Ford, *Today and Tomorrow*, 1926 (Reprinted by Productivity Press, Portland).
Taiichi Ohno, *Toyota Production System*, Productivity Press, Portland, OR, 1988
Spear and Bowen, 'Understanding the DNA of the Toyota Production System', *Harvard Business Review*, Sep/Oct 1999

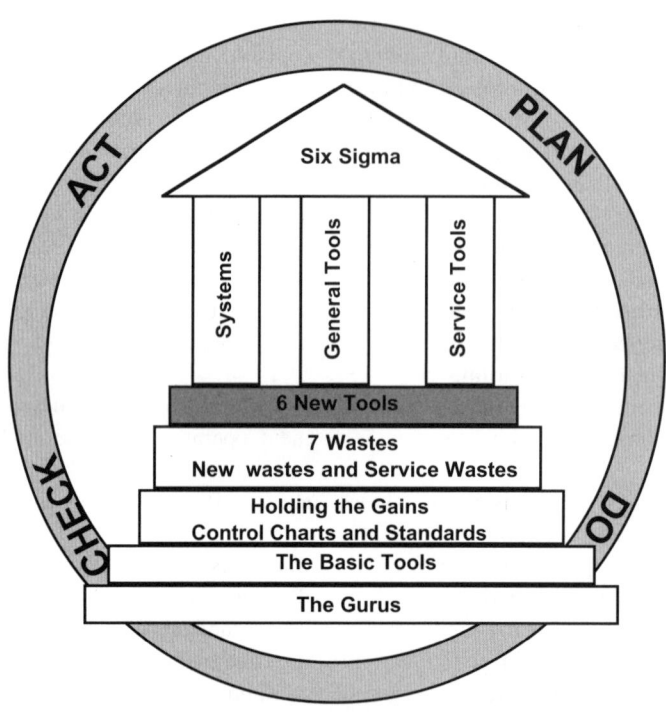

6 "New" Tools

**Affinity Diagram
Interrelationship or Network Diagram
Tree Diagram
Contingency Chart or Decision Tree
Matrix Analysis
Critical Path Analysis**

The New Tools

A working knowledge of the basic "7 Tools of Quality", described in a separate section, was considered by Ishikawa to be necessary for everyone. The "new" tools, described in this section, are not for everyone in the organisation, but should be useful to every manager, decision maker and team leader. The origin of the new 7 tools is unclear. Several have been around for a long time. But it was Mizuno who collected up seven and assembled them in a book entitled "The 7 New Quality Tools for Managers and Staff". The six new tools presented here are almost the same as those assembled by Mizuno and concentrate on the most useful ones. Like the basic 7 tools, the new tools should be thought of as a set, working together for maximum effectiveness.

The Affinity Diagram

The Affinity Diagram is a brainstorming aid used in group situations. The concept is a simple, but very effective. First a problem or issue is selected. This may be a specific issue or gut desire to improve. Then an appropriate group is assembled. A facilitator is appointed, ideally not a usual member of the group. The group brainstorms out suggestions by writing them on cards in silent generation mode. The cards are stuck up on a board. The group, now in discussion or in silent mode, works on assembling the cards into sets having an "affinity" with one another. Having rearranged and assembled them, a new card is added for each set with a brief description summarising the essential features of the group. So the output is a set of Summary Cards, one for each set of ideas. The end result is a clearer understanding of the issues involved or approaches that are possible. This tool should be used for idea generation and grouping, but not for detailed problem solving; the facilitator has to watch for this.

There seem to be several advantages: it is a participative exercise which generates commitment, it identifies commonalities in thinking within the group, and it provides a wealth of ideas which can be refined by using other tools. It is excellent for preliminary planning purposes, particularly in addressing ill-defined areas where the problem is to identify the problems. The group undertaking an Affinity Diagram task will often be an established team, but for some situations a special purpose group, ideally comprising a "diagonal slice" through the organisation, is required.

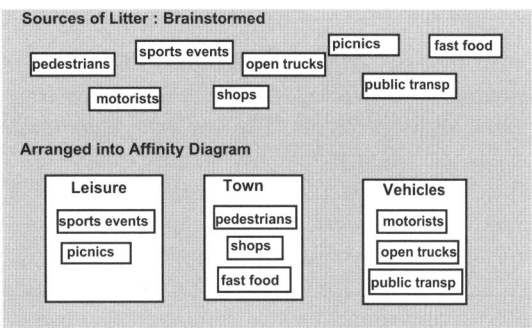

There is no one correct way, but a few suggestions follow :

- Use an external facilitator, with no "bones to pick"
- State the area clearly, even if it is not possible to state the problem
- Use 3M "Post-It" cards : one idea per card
- Have a silent generation period of 10 minutes
- Confine the card writing to a few words. Use verbs and nouns.
- Put the cards up on a flip chart in random order; don't preassemble
- Allow brief description of each idea but no discussion or criticism
- Let the facilitator assemble the first affinity sets without discussion
- Allow extra cards to be generated or cards to be rewritten
- In rearranging cards, don't allow arguments or long discussions
- It is worth spending time on the wording of Summary Cards
- Draw bold lines around the sets
- Keep the pace brisk; don't bog down in discussion.

Recently Gitlow has suggested the use of the "pictorial affinity diagram". Here, clusters of pictures rather than ideas are grouped. A leader develops a problem or mission. A suitable group is chosen. The group is given a set of pictures relating to a problem, product or service situation. The group is asked to assemble the pictures into clusters. This is done in silence. The group then discussses each cluster. The group is asked to develop a verbal description and these are placed on header cards. The idea is to name each cluster according to their "root cause effect". The clusters are transferred onto a large sheet of paper. A circle is drawn around each cluster and related clusters joined by lines. The result is the "pictorial affinity diagram". This method may be used to identify hitherto unrcognised themes, requirements or activities. For instance, what are the true attractions of a resort or theme park or university?

The Interrelationship or Network Diagram

An interrelationship diagram seeks to identify logical strings of connections between several problems or issues. The aim is to reach consensus about root causes, and about the sequence in which work should proceed. It helps prioritise areas to be tackled and avoids tackling inappropriate problems. People who have been involved with systems analysis will have already used this tool. So will project managers.

The tool can be used as a follow up from the generation of an Affinity Diagram. In this case, just begin where the team left off assembling the Affinity Diagram. There will already be logical groupings, so the task is to connect up the cards.

Alternatively, begin with a statement of the problem or issue or "Root Definition". Then brainstorm out the set of "minimum necessary activities" to address the problem or issue. Use a verb and noun in each activity. It's a good idea to use "Post-It" stickers; one per activity. Once again the task is to connect up the activities.

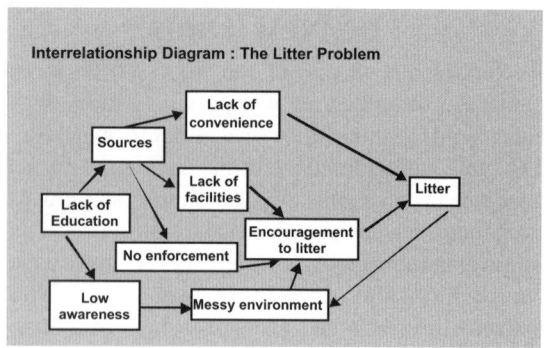

Interrelationship Diagram : The Litter Problem

Yet another possibility is project management. First consider the major elements to be completed. (This is called "chunking"). Connect up the major chunks first. Then take each major chunk and consider the detailed activities for each. Where a project network is being considered there will be only one ending point, and usually one start point. This is not necessarily the case with interrelationship diagrams. Use with CPA - see later.

Many connections will be obvious. There will be a logical sequence. But one can also tackle it in a more systematic way. For each activity ask
* which activities does the activity precede (draw an arrow to these activities)
* which activities does the activity follow (draw an arrow from these activities)
If the activities have been written on Post-It stickers, start a new diagram on a fresh sheet and reassemble stickers where the relationships exist.

Once you have completed the diagram examine it. Look out for activities where there are several arrows coming out. This would indicate an important root cause. These are obvious issues or problems to tackle first. Then look out for activities where there are several activities leading into them. This may indicate an important junction, milestone, or bottleneck that also requires serious attention.

Project managers know that the process of developing a network diagram is at least as important as doing the subsequent calculations to calculate the critical path (see the Project Network tool.) So it is with interrelationship diagrams in general. Having the team discuss the nature of the connections is a valuable educational task. Invariably the team will come away from the exercise feeling that they understand a lot more about the problem or issue. They will have much better ideas on how to tackle its solution or improvement. So for quality improvement in unstructured situations this is a very useful, but simple to use, tool.

The Tree Diagram

The Tree Diagram arranges goals, problems, or customer requirements in a hierarchy. It shows how a problem or goal is broken down into more detailed sub-problems or sub-goals. The breakdown into greater levels of detail can take place on several levels, until a manageable set of activities is achieved. It is similar to an organisation chart, or for those in manufacturing, like a bill of materials. That's it!

The Tree Diagram is another simple but effective tool. The only thing strange about it is the fact that it is not used more often. It helps to break down complex issues into sub issues. It is useful in planning a new program, a new service, or a new product. It is an essential part of constructing a Quality Function Deployment matrix (see the section on QFD) where it is used to assemble the "voice of the customer".

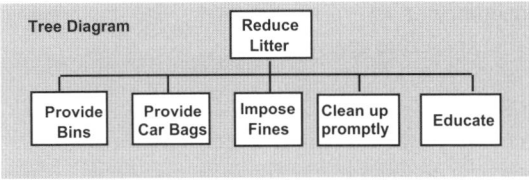

In constructing a Tree Diagram use a team. The same comments as for Affinity Diagrams apply. Start at the top, with the overriding goal or requirement. This is the first "parent" item. Then, layer by layer, consider what actions or activities or features are necessary to achieve the parent. What are the components (or child items) of the parent? When this is complete, consider each child item as a parent and repeat for the next layer. And so on. A rule of thumb is that there should no more than about 7 sub items (child items) for each parent item.

The Tree Diagram is related to the Affinity Diagram in as far as the statement of the original problem or issue may form the highest level item, the Summary Cards would be good candidates to form the first level, and a selection of cards from those brainstormed out would probably be used at various levels within a branch under each summary card.

The Tree Diagram is really another form of Interrelationship Diagram. The difference is that in a Tree Diagram each sub activity or goal has only one "parent" or main goal on the next highest level, whereas in the Interrelationship Diagram there is no such rule so that several interconnections are possible at each level. The Interrelationship Diagram is the spaghetti, but the Tree Diagram is a carefully layered dessert with the cherry on the top.

Perhaps the most difficult problem in assembling a tree diagram is to ensure that all items on each level are approximately at the same "level of resolution". So for example a "Total Quality Programme" would normally be found on a higher level than a "SPC Programme".

Contingency Chart or Decision Tree

The Contingency Chart helps to map the risks associated with the implementation of a plan. The chart looks similar to a Tree Diagram, except that on each layer all the alternatives to achieving the goal on the layer above are given. In the language used for the tree diagram, a parent is a statement of the goal and the child items are the alternatives. A child item on one level can also be a parent to levels below. Having established the tree, contingencies can be specifically considered.

Like much in project management the real value lies in the team-based process which considers alternatives beforehand. Too often project management concentrates on the mechanical aspects of activities and time, rather than on people and risk. The Contingency Chart helps to correct the balance. Both the Contingency Chart and the last of the new tools (discussed next) are necessary for good project management.

Managers familiar with decision theory will recognise that we are talking about a "decision tree". In a proper decision tree, however, probabilities are assigned to each option, and a calculation made as to the path of least cost. This degree of sophistication is not considered necessary in a Contingency Chart; in fact more emphasis is placed on thinking through the alternatives than in doing the calculations.

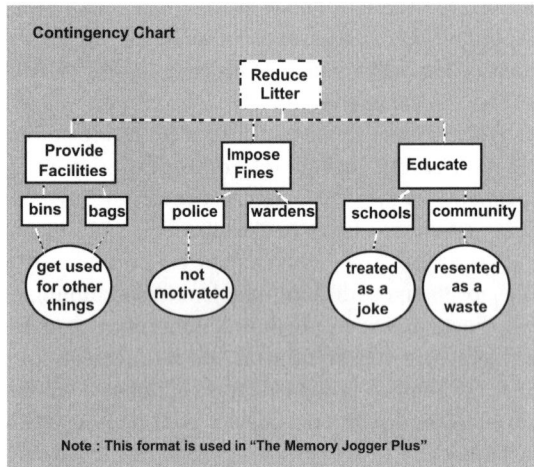

So the Contingency Chart amounts to sequential brainstorming followed by evaluation. Begin with the overall goal; write this at the top. Then the team brainstorms out alternative ways of getting there. These form the first level of the chart. Then each alternative is considered, and once again the team brainstorms out alternatives. These are written in under each major alternative. Continue in this way until the team considers that sufficient detail has been covered. This is normally two, or unusually three, levels down from the goal. An alternative to the first step is to list the major activities necessary to reach the goal. Thereafter the method proceeds as before.

After sufficient alternatives have been generated, a final level is brainstormed. This contains, for each alternative, a set of things that could go wrong or the more likely possibilities. Of course, there are many things that could go wrong, but the team should consider only major or most likely events. The difference between alternatives and things that can go wrong are that the former are choices under one's own control, but the latter are chance events or uncertainties. (The same distinction is found in decision trees).

Now the team should consider the consequences of each branch. What are the risks? What are the advantages? There are no rules how to do this; the value lies in the discussion. After discussion the best alternative should emerge, but the real value is having thought through the alternatives and their risks in advance. There should be few major unexpected events, and however the uncertainty turns out, the Contingency Chart should have ensured that most eventualities have been covered. "Forewarned is forearmed".

Matrix Analysis

Typically, problems in quality management have several "dimensions" or interacting aspects. For instance, the problem of litter requires at least education, litter bin provision, enforcement, cleanup, and bin clearing. The problem is then to sort them out, to rank them, to separate the "vital few from the trivial many" (to quote Juran). So Matrix Analysis is a set of tools for analysing data and for decision making. There are several tools ranging from simple to quite complex. A few of the most useful versions are looked at here. Matrix analysis can be used in conjunction with several of other of the "75", but notably QFD and value analysis.

Relative Weighting
A common way to weight or indicate relative importance is to merely distribute points between the factors under consideration. This is a "gut feel" procedure, common in market research and in customer focus groups. When done with a good sample of people (say above 30) it is possible to assign confidence limits to the results. A simple and useful technique.

A Matrix for Ranking Priorities : Pairwise Comparison
Pairwise comparison forces a more systematic consideration to be made, and therefore could be regarded as more reliable than point distribution. Of

course, pairwise comparison merely has a relative ranking as its outcome, not a relative weighting. Pairwise comparison typically follows an Affinity exercise or Tree Diagram exercise. The starting point is a set of actions or factors which need to rearranged into ranked order. Simply arrange the actions or factors to be ranked along two sides of a square matrix, with each side having the same actions. Give each factor or action a letter, just to make data entry easier. Mark the diagonal, from top left to bottom right. Then cross out all squares on the diagonal and all squares below the diagonal. You will left with a set of squares which enables each action to be compared with each other action. Now compare each action with each other action, pair by pair. Ask, firstly, for each pair, which action is the most important. If it is action A then write A in the square, and so on. If there is no clear difference or priority, leave the square blank. Repeat for all squares. Then, secondly, for all filled in squares, ask by how much does the chosen factor have priority over the second factor. If significantly different, give a score of 9 points. If only marginally, give a score of 3. Write the numbers in the squares. When all squares have been completed, add up the scores associated with each letter. The resulting scores represent the ranking. Very often you would find one or two really dominant actions or factors, and several with lower scores. This is normal and desirable. A Pareto analysis.

Two Dimensional Weighting

In, for example, Quality Function Deployment, but also in many other areas of quality management it is necessary to relate means to ends or "whats" to "hows". In QFD the "whats" are customer requirements and the "hows" are product features. To start, there will typically be a set of weighted or ranked "whats", derived by a method such as relative weighting. As for "hows", many product characteristics serve more than one purpose, for instance the meat in a hamburger provides nutrition, flavour, and bulk. The same can be said for a training programme which may provide skills, motivation and retain staff.

The problem is how to give weights or a ranking to the "hows", so that they reflect the "whats". Begin by constructing a matrix: whats in rows against hows in columns. The whats will usually be weighted, so add an extra column to reflect these weights. Now go through the matrix, cell by cell. For each, ask to what extent the how is able to meet the what. (eg. To what extent does the meat in a hamburger meet the requirement for nutrition?). The answer is high (write in 9 points), medium (write in 3 points), low (write in 1 point), or not at all (write in zero). In some cases a negative is possible (write in minus 3). Then, for each cell, multiply the point score by the weight for that row (i.e. for that "what"). Write this figure in the top right hand of the cell. Lastly, add up the top right hand figures for each column (i.e. for each "how"). This gives a weighting which reflects the ability of each "how" to meet each "what".

Example : Design of a Hamburger to Customer preferences

Begin with a Focus Group to determine Customer Requirements and relative weightings. Then :

Customer Requirements	Customer preference weighting	Features		
		Beef	Bun	Lettuce
Moisture	1	0 / 0	0 / 1	1 / 9 / 9
Flavour	3	27 / 9	0 / 0	0 / 3 / 9
Nutrition	3	27 / 9	9 / 3	0 / 0 / 0
Visual Appeal	5	45 / 9	5 / 1	5 / 1 / 5
Value for Money	5	45 / 9	5 / 1	0 / 1 / 5
Weighted scores		144	19	6 28

Conclusion : Concentrate attention on Beef and Ketchup

Note : This is the analysis performed in a QFD Matrix

The applications of this method are very wide. Apart from product design through QFD, other applications are selecting what sub-programmes are to be implemented as part of a Six Sigma programme, selecting suppliers, and selecting between several locations for a new factory.

Multi Dimensional Matrices

Multi Dimensional Matrices are a whole class of matrices which allow data to be analysed in several dimensions. Of course, strictly a matrix can compare only two factors at a time, but the inclusion of additional factors can add insight.

Two Dimensional matrices can show, for example, defects against operator; or complaints against shift.

Three Dimensional matrices can show defects against operator and time; or complaints against shift and location.

Four Dimensional matrices can show defects against operator and time as well as giving additional data relating to products; or complaints against shift and location as well as giving additional data on tasks performed.

In all cases the cells of the matrices can contain numerical data or symbols to indicate high, medium, low or nil.

Critical Path Analysis

The last of the "new" tools is particularly relevant for project management. Of course, project management is not unique to Quality Management, but without good project management the implementation of Total Quality or Six Sigma is impossible.

Critical Path Analysis (CPA) is a long established tool for project management. Project Management is a vital part of any quality implementation and is often fairly poorly managed. CPA is useful to schedule resource usage in any environment. Today there is abundant inexpensive software for CPA and its extensions, and you should seldom need to calculate a network. But be warned: DO NOT get carried away by sophisticated software; most features will not be required. And DO use the Contingency Chart in conjunction with CPA.

CPA aims at establishing the time needed for a project, what the critical activities are, and what the expected start and finish times are for each activity. It uses a network of arrows or nodes to establish the logical order of activities. The real value of CPA is in drawing the network, not in the subsequent calculations.

(The method to be described below is known as "activity on node". This is becoming the standard. An older alternative is known as "activity on arrow". In the latter case "dummy" activities are sometimes required. Detail is to be found in numerous textbooks, if you require it.)

CRITICAL PATH ANALYSIS (CPA)

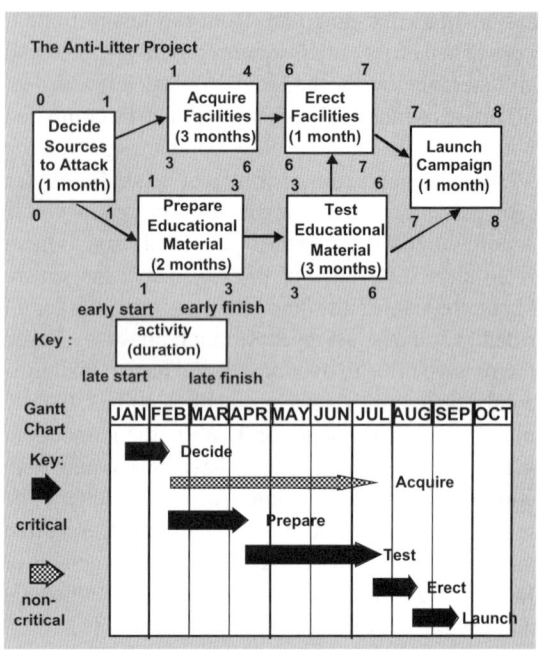

Begin by listing all the activities (verb plus noun) that are necessary for the project. Try to keep these at a high level; you can add sub-networks later. Post-it stickers are a good idea for flexibility. Each activity should have an estimated time. Put each activity in a square. Then arrange the activities into logical order by connecting them up with arrows. The rule is: no activity can start before its predecessor activity is complete. If activities can run in parallel do not arrange them in sequence. There should be one start activity and one end activity and no circular loops. Recall that getting the network right (i.e. thinking through the project in advance) is the major benefit. Use a team if possible.

To calculate times, a CPA network requires a "forward pass" and a "backward pass"; both are simple.

Begin the forward pass at time 0. This is the "early start" time for the first activity. "Early start" is the earliest time that an activity can start; "early finish" is the earliest time that an activity can be completed by, and is equal to the early start time plus the duration of the activity. Write in the early start time of each activity on the top left hand corner of the activity square, and the early finish time on the top right hand of the square. The early finish of each activity becomes the early start time of the next activity. Where there are two or more immediate predecessor activities, take the greater of the finish dates of the predecessors because all must be complete before the activity can begin. Move through the whole network doing this calculation activity by activity. The early finish of the last activity is the minimum project duration.

Now begin the backward pass. The early finish of the last activity will also be the "late finish" of that activity ("late finish" is the latest time that an activity can finish by whilst not delaying the completion of the entire project. "late start" is the latest time that an activity can start without delaying the whole project. Write in the late finish on the bottom right hand of each activity square, and the late start on the bottom left of the activity square.) Begin with the late finish time for the last activity. The late start for each activity equals the late finish minus the duration. Now move backwards through the network. The late start of an activity becomes the late finish of its predecessor activity in all cases except where there are two or more immediate subsequent activities. In this case take the smaller of late start dates of the immediate subsequent activities as the late finish for the activity. (Since there are several subsequent activities it is the earliest of the late starts that will govern). At the end of the backward pass you should end with a late start time for the first activity of zero; if not you have made a mistake.

You have now established, for each activity, the "early start". "early finish", "late start", and "late finish". The "slack" or additional free time for each activity equals (late finish - early finish) or (late start - early start). These should give the same result. Some activities, forming a continuous path through the network, will have zero slack. This is the critical path. Any delay along the critical path will delay the whole project; it follows that these are the activities to monitor most closely.

To aid communication, it is a good idea to show the planned early start, early finish and late finish dates on a bar chart for each activity.

As the project proceeds, monitor progress, update the times, update the network if necessary, and redo the calculation. It is nice to have a computer to do this for you.

Further reading:
Shigeru Mizuno (ed), *Management for Quality Improvement: The 7 New QC Tools*, Productivity Press, 1988
Michael Brassard, *The Memory Jogger Plus*, GOAL/QPC, 1989
Howard S. Gitlow, "Learning about a Loved One: The Quality Management Approach", *Quality Engineering*, 13(1), September 2000, pp 115-119 (about pictorial affinity diagrams).

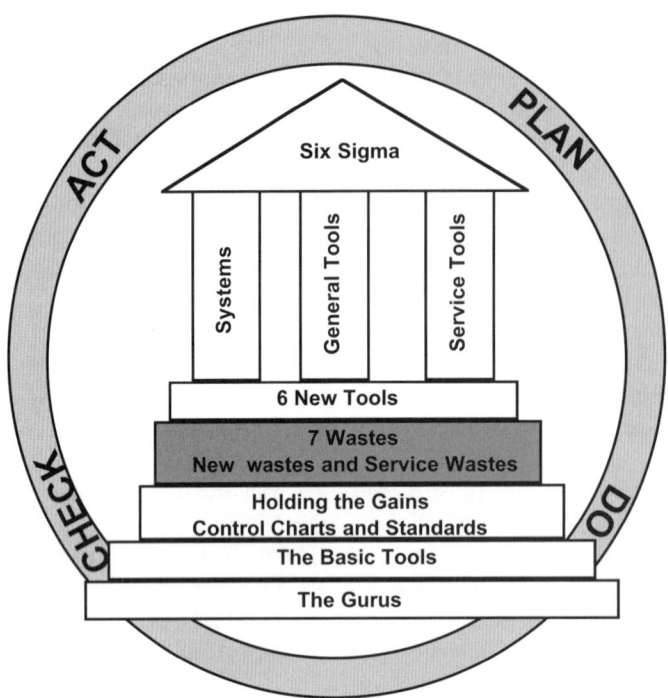

The 7 Wastes

Overproduction
Waiting
Transporting
Inappropriate Processing or "Overprocessing"
Unnecessary Inventory
Unnecessary Motion
Defects

New Wastes
Making the Wrong Product Correctly
Untapped Human Potential
Inappropriate Systems and Information
Waste Energy

Service Wastes
Delay
Duplication
Movement
Unclear Communication
Wrong Inventory
Lost Customer Opportunities
Errors

The 7 Wastes

The "7 Wastes" or MUDA were originally developed by Toyota's chief engineer Taiichi Ohno to neatly encapsulate all the forms of waste that occur in a manufacturing plant. Identification of waste is the first stage to its elimination. Now we recognize that use of the 7 wastes extends into service and distribution. It was Deming who pointed out that to improve quality it is necessary to reduce waste. Continually.

The 7 wastes are productivity- rather than quality-related. But quality and productivity are closely linked. Improved productivity leads to leaner operations which make quality problems more visible. And better quality improves productivity by cutting out wasteful practices such as rework, extra inspection, and all the activities associated with doing an operation for the second time. So a systematic attack on wastes is also a systematic attack on some of the underlying causes of poor quality. By reducing waste we get to work "smarter" rather than "harder". More for less: its got to be good!

The opposite of waste is value adding. By definition, any activity that does not add value for the customer is waste and should be a candidate for reduction or elimination. We can classify activities into value adding, non value adding, and non value adding but temporarily necessary. The last two are waste. Value adding activities may be to do with the present or the future.

The 7 wastes are a set rather than individual entities. As a set they form the core of the just-in-time or lean philosophy, and as such they have been the subject of awareness training for operators in manufacturing. Checklists have often been developed from them. At Toyota there are waste checklists for manufacturing, distribution, and clerical operations.

You can remember the seven wastes by asking, "Who is TIM WOOD?" Answer: Transport, Inventory, Motion, Waiting, Overproduction, Over-processing, and Defects. (This idea came from the Lean Office at Cooper Standard, Plymouth, UK.)

The Waste of Overproduction

Ohno believed that the waste of overproduction was the most serious of all the wastes because it was the root of so many problems. Overproduction is making too much, too early or "just-in-case". It is working ahead of the production schedule, which in turn should be linked to the customer's rate of demand. The aim should be to make exactly what is required, no more and no less, just-in-time and with perfect quality. Overproduction discourages a smooth flow of goods or services. "Lumpiness" (i.e. making products or working in erratic bursts) is a force against quality and productivity. By contrast, regularity encourages a "no surprises" atmosphere which may not be very exciting but is much better management.

Overproduction leads directly to excessive lead time and storage time and storage cost. As a result defects may not be detected early, products may deteriorate, and artificial pressures on work rate may be generated. All these increase the chances of defects. Taking it further, overproduction leads to excessive work-in-process inventories which lead to the physical separation of operations and the discouragement of communication.

Yet overproduction is often the natural state. People do not have to be encouraged to overproduce; they often do so "just to be safe". Often this is reinforced by a bonus system that encourages output that is not needed. By contrast, the Kanban system prevents unplanned overproduction by allowing work to move forwards only when the next work area is ready to receive it. Although kanban was made famous in manufacturing, it was originally developed from the supermarket restocking procedure and certainly has application in the service industry. (Hamburgers are only made at a rate in line with demand and clerical operations are most effective when there is a uniform flow of work.) The motto "sell daily? make daily!" is as relevant in an office as it is in a factory. In Lean we talk about "EPE" - every product every - to emphasize regularity and avoid overproduction.

The Waste of Waiting

The waste of waiting occurs whenever time is not being used effectively. Time is an important element of competitiveness and quality. Customers do not appreciate being kept waiting but they may be prepared to pay a premium to be dealt with faster. Waiting involves a delay to value adding activities.

In a factory, any time that materials or components are seen to be not moving (or not having value added) is an indication of waste. Waiting is the enemy of smooth flow. Although it may be very difficult to reduce waiting to zero, the goal remains. Whether the waiting is of parts in a factory or customers in a bank there should always be an awareness of a non-ideal situation and a questioning of how the situation can be improved. Waiting interrupts the rhythm of work.

When operators and employees are waiting for work or simply waiting for something to do, it is waste. Can the time not be better spent on another operation or on training, cleaning, maintaining, checking, practising changeovers or even deliberate relaxation? All of these are forces for improved quality and productivity. But they require management to have developed a contingency plan on the best use of time.

A bottleneck operation that is waiting for work is a waste. As Goldratt has pointed out in his book "The Goal", "an hour lost at a bottleneck is an hour lost for the whole plant". Effective use of bottleneck time is a key to regular production which in turn strongly influences productivity and quality.

And of course don't keep customers waiting. Sooner or later they will leave, and you will get to feel the pain.

The Waste of Transporting

Customers do not pay to have goods moved around (unless they have hired a removal service!). So any movement of materials in a factory is waste. It is a waste that can never be fully eliminated but it is also a waste that over time should be continually reduced. The number of transport and material handling operations is directly proportional to the likelihood of damage and deterioration. Double handling is a waste that affects productivity and quality.

Transporting is closely linked to communication. Where distances are long, communication is discouraged and quality may be the victim. Feedback on poor quality is inversely related to transportation length, whether in manufacturing or in services. There is increasingly the awareness that for improved quality in manufacturing or services, people from interacting groups need to be located physically closer together. For instance, the design office may be placed deliberately near the production area.

When this waste gains recognition by employees steps can be taken to reduce it. Measures include monitoring the flow lengths of products through a factory or paper through an office. The number of steps, and in particular the number of non value-adding steps, should be monitored. (This can be used as an input into various techniques such as value analysis, nominal group, or time charting.)

A very useful exercise is to do a "spaghetti" diagram, tracing movement on a diagram of the layout. This works in offices and factories. And don't forget to do a spaghetti diagram on customer movement.

The Waste of Inappropriate Processing or "Overprocessing"

Inappropriate processing refers to the waste of "using a hammer to crack a nut". Thinking in terms of one big machine instead of several smaller ones discourages operator "ownership", leads to pressure to run the machine as often as possible rather than only when needed, and encourages general purpose machines that may not be ideal for the need at hand. It also leads to poor layout, which as we have seen in the previous section, leads to extra transportation and poor communication. So the ideal is to use the smallest machine, capable of producing the required quality, distributed to the points of use.

Inappropriate processing refers to machines and processes that are not quality capable. In other words, a process that cannot help but make defects. (The concept of capability is dealt with more fully in the section on "holding the gains".) In general, a capable process requires to have the correct methods, training, and tools, as well as having the required standards clearly known.

Inappropriate processing also refers to people who are not "quality capable" of doing the job required of them. If that is so, why is it so? Is it due to motivation or inability or unclear communication?

The Waste of Unnecessary Inventory

Although having no inventory is a goal that can never be attained, inventory is the enemy of quality and productivity. This is so because inventory tends to increase leadtime, prevents rapid identification of problems, and increases space thereby discouraging communication. The true cost of extra inventory is very much in excess of the money tied up in it.

Lean (or JIT) manufacturing has taught that inventory deliberately hides problems by covering them up. So, perhaps, a quality problem is not considered important because there are always extra parts available if one is defective. Lean encourages deliberate inventory reduction to uncover this sort of problem. Perhaps the safety inventory is deliberately cut. If nothing happens - fine, you have learned to operate with a leaner system. If stoppage occurs - good, because the problem has been recognized and can now be attacked at its root cause. (See the 5 Why technique on how this is done.)

The Waste of Unnecessary Motions

Unnecessary motions refers to the importance of ergonomics for quality and productivity. If operators have to stretch, bend, pick-up, move in order to see better, or in any way unduly exert themselves, the victim is immediately the operator but ultimately quality and productivity.

This is why an awareness of the ergonomics of the workplace is not only ethically desirable, but economically sound. Toyota, famous for its quality, is known to place a high importance on "quality of work life". Toyota encourages all its employees to be aware of working conditions that contribute to this form of waste.

It is sometimes instructive to make videos of both operators and customers. For instance, in a bistro a video may reveal that an assistant could serve coffee and cake in half the time with a little thought. Hotter and more consistent coffee would result, and customers would enjoy faster service. Get the operators themselves to make the video and to watch it. And in a bank make a video of customers searching for forms and pens.

At work, in factory or office, this waste is strongly related to safety. Remove unsafe acts and unsafe conditions. Audit for "near misses".

The Waste of Defects

Last, but not least, is the waste of defects. This one was included by Ohno to complete the set, and is the "bottom line". Defects cost money. Just how much is discussed under the technique of Cost of Quality. The Toyota philosophy is that a defect should be regarded as a challenge, as an opportunity to improve, rather than something to be traded off against what is ultimately poor management. That a defect, any defect, is a waste has much in common with the uncompromising "zero defect" view of Phil Crosby.

Further reading
Japan Management Association, Kanban : *Just-in-Time at Toyota*, Productivity Press, 1985
Maasaki Imai, *Gemba Kaizen*, McGraw Hill, 1997, Chapter 6
Goldratt and Cox, *The Goal*, STG

New Wastes.

Various authors have extended Ohno's list. Here are a few:

* The *Waste of Making the Wrong Product* (correctly). Womack and Jones have suggested this. It relates back to their first principle of Lean Thinking "The critical starting point for Lean Thinking is Value" (page 16) and value "begins with the ultimate customer". Today this is also the starting point of ISO 9001:2000.

* The *Waste of Untapped Human Potential*. Ohno was reported to have said that the real objective of the Toyota Production System was "to create thinking people". So this "new" waste links directly back to the original seven. Human potential does not just need to be set free. It requires clear communication, commitment, and support.

* The *Waste of Inappropriate Systems and Information*. This also has its origins in Lean Thinking and Business Processes. Don't automate waste. Go for the most simple, visible system. As Michael Hammer has said, "don't automate, obliterate"

* *Waste Energy*. This is not merely a question of being green, but reduction makes increasing economic sense. But beyond this, wasting energy such as leaving lights and printers switched on overnight is symptomatic of wider malaise.

Seven Service Wastes

Most of the above wastes are seen from the organisations perspective. What about the customer's perspective? Perhaps a quality improvement programme should begin with the service wastes:

* *Delay:* on the part of customers waiting for service, for delivery, in queues, for response, not arriving as promised. The customer's time may seem free to the provider, but when she goes elsewhere the pain begins.

* *Duplication:* having to re-enter data, repeat details on forms, copy information across, answer queries from several sources within the same organisation.

* *Unnecessary Movement:* queuing several times, lack of one-stop, poor ergonomics in the service encounter.

* *Unclear Communication,* and the wastes of seeking clarification, confusion over product or service use, wasting time finding a location which may result in misuse or duplication.

* *Incorrect Inventory:* out-of-stock, unable to get exactly what was required, substitute products or services.

* *Opportunity Lost* to retain or win customers, failure to establish rapport, ignoring customers, unfriendliness, rudeness.

* *Errors*: in the service transaction, product defects in the product-service bundle, lost or damaged goods.

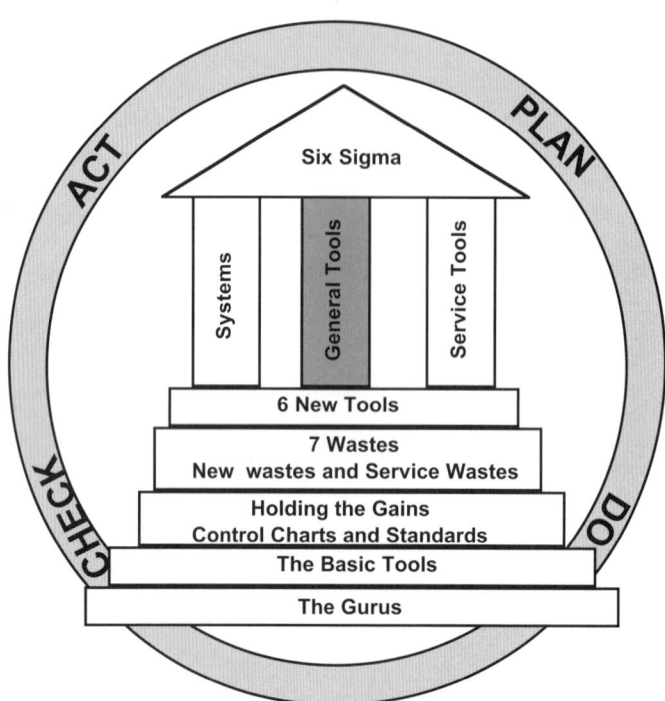

General Tools

in alphabetical order

5S

The 5S's stem from five Japanese words. However, there are English equivalents that more or less mean the same thing. One is Sort, Simplify, Sweep, Standardise, Self Discipline. Some prefer the 5 C variant of Cleanup, Configure, Clean and check, Conformity, Custom and practice. Sometimes a sixth S is added for Safety.

At first glance, 5S is about good housekeeping. It is, but it goes much further. It is really about changing the mindset, about making orderly and standardised operations the norm rather than the exception. The 5 S concept is one of the cornerstones of Quality and Lean Management and has had a long association with the Shingo and the Toyota Production System (where, however, it is known as the 4S system). It is fundamental to both TPM and to total quality, and has almost invariably been the first programme undertaken by Japanese companies in the UK when taking over operations in a British factory. 5S has a direct impact on safety, cost, quality, delivery, and on OEE.

Here we adopt a Western version, origin unknown, called CANDO whilst still referring to the concept as "5S".

C is for Cleanup. This is about removing all items (especially accumulated dirt and grime, but also inventory, paper, furniture, tools, memos, manuals, rubbish, filing cabinets, etc) that are not required or are unnecessary within a period ahead. Such items are waste, or lead to waste. They take up space, lead to extra walking around, and lead to waste of time whilst searching for needed items buried under piles of less important material. An office example is the "clean desk" policy run by several companies, requiring employees to have a clear desk at the end of each day. In the office beware of paperwork that is shuffled, reread, and searched through often several times per day. It's all waste. Cleanout also includes fixing: any tools or equipment that is broken or not calibrated must either be thrown away or repaired - decide which, and act.

There are two approaches. One is to begin with a longer period (say 6 months) and to clear all that is not foreseen to be used within that period; then to reduce the period until you are working with only (say) this week's items. The more common approach is to "red tag" items that are not in use or where there is uncertainty. Dates are written on the red tags. Tagged items are then removed and either thrown out or, where there is uncertainty about the future use of the item, placed in a holding area. Tagged items remaining in the holding area for more than say 6 months are thrown out. Red tagging is best done by in focused areas, one at a time. "Blitz" one area, then move on. Red tagging should also be done by both operators from the area, who should be issued with say 4 red tags and challenged to use them up, and by red tag pairs comprising a supervisor from the area and an outsider. Cleanup is also an opportunity to review the floor paint layout and policy. Are the aisles in the right place bearing in mind the requirements for flow, are the colours used appropriate, and so forth. Finally don't forget to include windows, walls (are those posters still appropriate?), lighting, and the overhead beams and roof.

A is for Arranging; "a place for everything". This step aims to arrange the workplace and its associated tools, equipment and inventory in the optimal locations. The analogy between the kitchen and the garage is often used. In the kitchen, cutlery is kept in specific slots in a specific drawer; in the garage tools, rags, and half used tins of paint often lie around for ages. The goal is to make the workplace not only good and easy to work in, but also that anyone should be able to locate the necessary equipment. Reaching, bending and walking should be minimised. It is really about having things easy to hand, labelled, classified, and easily visible. Time wasted should be cut by careful location of tools and materials. Do a Pareto in order to locate the most frequently used items closest. It may be possible to incorporate some failsafing: cords attached to tools, racking or slots that do not hold other than the correct tool.

Instructions and standards should be clear (drawings better than words), up to date, and be located at the workplace. Shadow boards may be used for tools, books arranged by topic, shelves not too high, wheels on carts for changeover equipment, heavy low and light high, colour coded connections and pipes, and so on. It is also about inventory: having specific locations or footprints for specific parts, perhaps painted squares, minimum and maximum quantities shown, and of course a limit on excessive parts delivered lineside too early. When combined with cleanup, this lays the foundation for the kanban system. Taking arrangement further means thinking about overhead "Andon" boards, signalling systems, progress boards, charts and graphs, and establishing responsibility for them being kept up to date. A major consideration should be consideration of the correct size for pallets and boxes, and the arrangements for their movement so as to avoid double handling.

N is for Neatness; "everything in its place" and ready to go. The simple fact is that the cleaner or tidier a location is, the easier it is to see if something is out of place. Once again, the garage analogy; in a clean garage an oil leak is seen straight away. Neatness has a direct impact on productivity: searching for lost papers and tools should be eliminated. It is also a safety issue.

Responsibility for Neatness should lie with the operator, not with cleaners. Good 5S programmes establish what are termed "5 Minute Cleanup" routines. Here, each operator develops his or her own 5 minute per day clean and check routine, for each day of the week. Note that this is not left to chance; it is a carefully timed and documented set of actions that are to be undertaken on specific days of the week. The documentation, of course, should be kept at the workplace and should for instance specify what abnormality looks like and what cleaning agents should be used.

Neatness and cleanliness extends to non-seen areas: machines need to be clean inside and out - in fact, making the innards of machines visible by using transparent covers is desirable. Routine maintenance may be incorporated: oil every day, replace after 5000 sheets, and "aircraft style checks" where items are checked at the start of every shift (have you ever been into a bank to discover a non-working pen chained to the counter?). One important activity is identifying which maintenance activities are the responsibility of the ordinary staff, and which are the responsibilities of specialist maintenance staff. Responsibility for the photocopier is good example; clearly define who is responsible for what: secretaries, staff, specialists.

D is for "Discipline". This step aims to keep the factory or office in a "Chief Executive's visit" state all the time. The thought here is that it is easier to keep things going, than to stop and restart over again - like the momentum of a train. This is not discipline in the army sense, but rather getting into the routine or mindset of keeping up the standards and procedures established in earlier steps. The difficulty of achieving this should not be underestimated; Toyota reckons it takes several months to establish this with a new employee. So what is required to keep up the momentum? First, a regular audit. It is a good idea to establish a 5S committee of operators themselves and get them to establish the audit checklist. But remember to include the not-so-obvious: clothing, corners, waste bins, stairways, windows, signs, electrical connections, as well as the obvious machines, jigs, and stores. The audit time should be at random intervals. The audit checklist should not be used only as weekly pat on the back, but as a means of detecting any deterioration, and the reasons for that deterioration. But rewards and recognition, both intrinsic and extrinsic, are also part of the game. Intrinsic rewards include recognition of good work, perhaps by a weekly "floating trophy" and built into staff evaluations, and extrinsic rewards may include small prizes or vouchers. Much would depend on company culture.

Finally, **O stands for Ongoing Improvement.** This is maintaining the tempo of continuous improvement. Here we should not only be concerned with cleaning up spillage of oil and so forth, but asking why the spillage occurred in the first place. Get to the root cause. This is Juran's views on "chronic" and "sporadic" defects; whilst it is OK to tackle sporadic defects by fire fighting, an attack on the underlying and continuing sources of defects means that the improvements go on and on and on. How do we move towards this? First, by establishing clear standards so one can move from standard to standard. Second, by a continuing Pareto attack on the recurring sources of problems, which means having records to do this. Third, by tightening the red tag horizon. Fourth, by seeking pokayoke in regard to housekeeping; for example machines that will not start before routine checks have been made or audible warnings that activate if bar codes are not scanned. And we also need to repeat the Cleanup activity at regular intervals because products and tooling changes. Most of all we need to encourage a questioning culture combined with visibility - so that if something is out of place or missing it is not only noticed, but also questioned. This takes years of management persistence.

Further reading
Hiroyuki Hirano, *5 Pillars of the Visual Workplace*, Productivity Press, Portland, 1995

The "Five Whys" and Root Cause Problem Solving

The 5 whys is a technique to ensure that the root causes of problems are sought out. It simply requires that the user asks "why?" several times over. The technique is called the "5 whys" because it is the experience of its inventor, the Toyota company, that "why" needs to be asked successively five times before the root cause is established.

This simple but very effective technique really amounts to a questioning attitude. Never accept the first reason given; always probe behind the answer. It goes along with the philosophy that a defect or problem is something precious; not to be wasted by merely solving it, but taking full benefit by exposing the underlying causes that have led to it in the first place. Many (for instance the MIT study on the worldwide car industry) believe that it is this unrelenting seeking out of root causes that have given the Japanese motor industry the edge on quality, reliability and productivity.

An example follows: A door does not appear to close as well as it should. Why? Because the alignment is not perfect. Why? Because the hinges are not always located in exactly the right place. Why? Because, although the robot that locates the hinge has high consistency, the frame onto which it is fixed is not always resting in exactly the same place. Why? Because the overall unit containing the frame is not stiff enough. Why? Because stiffness of the unit during manufacture does not appear to have been fully accounted for. So the real solution is to look at the redesign of the unit for manufacture.

Perhaps there are even more whys. Why did this happen in the first place? (Insufficient cooperation between design and manufacturing.) Why so? (It was a rushed priority.) Why? (Marketing had not given sufficient notice.) Why? And so on.

A variation of the 5 Why technique is the "5 How" technique. This is often used in tracing the cause of a failure in a product or in service delivery. ("How did that happen?"....) The thinking and procedure is exactly the same.

Root Cause Problem Solving

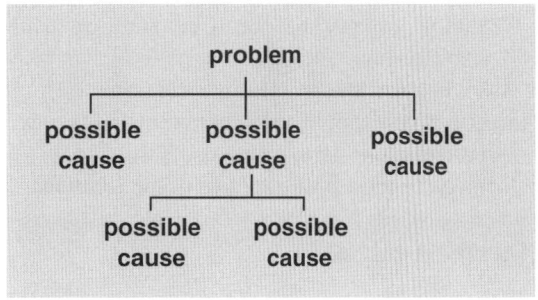

The emphasis on "root cause" problem solving is fundamental to the philosophies of JIT, lean manufacturing, continuous improvement, the Toyota production system, and TQM. It means solving problems at the root rather than at the superficial or immediately obvious levels. But how do you get to the root cause? In the following sections two technique are examined. But first, we should look at the whole concept of root cause analysis.

In a thoughtful article Finlow-Bates concludes that there are no ultimate root causes. Rather, root causes are dependent upon the problem owner; there can be more than one potential root cause and that the final choice of root cause cannot be made until the economics of possible solutions have been considered. He illustrates the point by the example of a delivery failure. The root cause for the customer is that the parcel is late. The root cause for the delivery company is that the problem delivery failure was due to the van not starting which can be traced to the root cause of a leaking underground tank. For the tank supplier the root cause was a failure in the solder. For the solder supplier the root cause was …. Each person along the chain is not interested in the problems of lower echelons. Each of these causes represents a failure in control or in communication. The real issue is therefore not what is the root cause, but how can the problem be (temporarily?) solved most economically and effectively to prevent recurrence.

Finlow-Bates suggests following **six steps:**
* What is the unwanted effect? (Finlow-Bates suggests two words; subject and deviation, for example parcels late)
* What is the direct physical cause?
* Follow the direct physical line of the cause. For example, parcels late, van won't start, etc. This establishes the "staircase"
* Ask who owns the problem at each stage.
* Identify where should one intervene in the staircase to effect a long-term solutions.
* Identify the most cost-effective of the solutions.

Barrier Analysis

Barrier Analysis (Wilson et al) may be used where implementation problems are being experienced. It amounts to a straightforward set of questions that are addressed to an unwanted problem or event:

* What are the threats, hazards or potential problems that can influence the situation? Threats may be physical or psychological, or influence status, security, or self esteem.
* Who or what are the "Targets" for change? In any change there will be victims and beneficiaries, some perhaps unintended. It is useful to list these. The target may be human, animal, organisation, environment, group, team, family, or other.
* What are the barriers? These may be physical, geographic, communication, language, culture, administrative, organisational. Also, what are the safeguards that are supposed to be in place to make the change easier or more acceptable, and if they are not in place, why are they not. Should the threat be isolated, or should the target be isolated, or both?
* What is the "Trace". That is, what is the sequence of events or history that has lead up to this situation? Real or imaginary.

Further reading:
T Finlow-Bates, "The Root Cause Myth", *The TQM Magazine*, Volume 10 Number 1, 1998, pp10-15
The following book has some useful material in relation to the last section:
Paul Wilson, Larry Dell, Gaylord Anderson, *Root Cause Analysis: A Tool for Total Quality Management*, ASQC Quality Press, Milwaukee, WI, 1993

Six Honest Working Men and Is Is-not Analysis

Rudyard Kipling's "Six Honest Serving Men" remains, some 100 years after it was first written, one of the most useful problem analysis tools. The original verse is,

"I knew six honest serving men, they taught me all I knew; their names are what and why and when, and where and how and who".

Such a simple little verse; so much wisdom – so often ignored!

The six men are a very useful way of defining customers, their requirements and what is really valued. In the opinion of the author it's a pity that the six men is not the first call of marketeers rather than the "marketing mix" or 4 P's (product, price, place, promotion).

The six men can also be usefully combined with Is Is-Not analysis first put forward (it is believed) by

Kepner-Tregoe. This helps clarify what is, and what is not the issue, and so on:

	Is	Is Not	So...
What (Why)	Lectures	Tutorials	
When	Start Time	Finish Time	
Where	Too cold	Seats	
Who (How)	John	Norman	

Benchmarking

The Benchmarking Centre defines Benchmarking as "the continuous, systematic search for, and implementation of, best practices which lead to superior performance". In essence it aims to compare the performance of critical processes with leading achievers. It is a guideline to what is necessary in present performance and to future requirements if the organization is to be "world class". It is about knowing yourself and really knowing the competition - where they are weak, where they are strong, and where they are going. To an extent, benchmarking is an alternative to "cost plus" budgeting, and to productivity targeting by simply "matching inflation". It is outward looking rather than inward looking. It is concerned with tracking performance, not just taking snapshots. Think of the ongoing Deming Cycle. And like several other techniques discussed here it is equally applicable to products and to services.

Of course, benchmarking is not new. People and organizations have always compared themselves to others. Juran quotes the example of how, early in the 20th century, German generals visited the Barnum and Bailey circus to study the world-renowned methods it used to move materials and animals from city to city. But it was the Xerox corporation that appears to have pioneered "competitive benchmarking". It was the systematic and comprehensive way in which Xerox set about making benchmarking a competitive weapon that has brought this technique into prominence. Robert Camp of Xerox is responsible for much of the thinking, and has written the definitive book.

Types of benchmarking include Internal (where one branch is compared with others - see the section on Best Demonstrated Practice), Competitive (as per Xerox, comparing with the toughest competitors), Functional (where similar processes are compared inside of your industry but not with direct competitors - say room service in two non-competing hotels), Generic or Process (where basic processes found in any business, such as recruitment or billing, are compared), and Performance (where measures (typically on cost, quality, delivery, reliability, and response) are compared.

Benchmarking can be seen not just as a technique on its own, but as one of a mutually reinforcing family. The insights from benchmarking are useful if not necessary for quality function deployment. For value management it can help identify what is technically possible. It is powerful as a force for change when used in force field analysis. It identifies on which of Garvin's dimensions of quality a competitor is competing. And systematic measurement is part of any quality improvement process, such as the Deming cycle or the Juran Trilogy.

We begin with the understanding that a single measure of performance is rarely adequate. Just as several instruments are necessary to monitor and control the performance of a car or plane, so it is with any organization. Now recognize that to be competitive in quality and productivity, steady inward-looking progress may not be enough. But of course one does not go out to benchmark everything possible. It must be a directed search. Robert Camp proposes using a process control model (involving inputs, process, outputs, feedback, and results) and suggests that all these are benchmarking candidates, and that "step zero", where time and care is spent considering the purpose of the exercise is most important. Camp has a 10 step approach covering planning (covering what, whom, and how), analysis (where the current and future gaps are determined), integration (involving communication and revision of goals), action (where actions are developed, then monitored, and benchmarks recalibrated).

What to measure

Robert Camp states that benchmarking is "first a goal setting process". You have to know what to benchmark, and, as with much of quality management, this brings you right back to the customer. Identify who are your customers, present and future. Now you can begin to assess their needs and the necessary core processes. These are the areas where the organization absolutely needs to perform well, and areas where unique advantages can be obtained. (Garvin's dimensions are useful as an aid). The areas can be assembled by a team using the nominal group technique (see the section on NGT) and the Affinity Diagram (see the New Tools).

There may be a particular interest in targeting areas that are known to be important, such as costs or complaints or geographical areas. Staff policies, salaries, and personnel policies on training, recruitment, and the use of people at work may be relevant. There may well be some standard productivity or quality measures in the industry. Beware of being too specific on what should be measured - there may be "more than one way to skin a cat". The idea is to concentrate on processes first and measures of performance second. With what it is you wish to benchmark now known, the next step is to identify who to benchmark.

It is a good idea to think through the information collection procedure, in particular who will be responsible and where will it be centred. The latter has to be clearly communicated so that if information is obtained from or by an unexpected source, it will still go to the right place. It will often be necessary to dedicate people, part time or short term, to information collection.

Who to measure

The aim of competitive benchmarking is to find the "industry best" performance, and where appropriate the "world best" performance. The toughest competitors now and in future are often known or easy to short-list, so a search can be more focused. But do not close minds to the possibility of world class performance from a new or unexpected source. Benchmarking is an ongoing process. In Xerox, benchmarking is known of throughout the company and a "little red book" on benchmarking has been widely issued. For non competitive benchmarking the services of organisations such as the Benchmarking Centre can be used to pinpoint benchmarking partners.

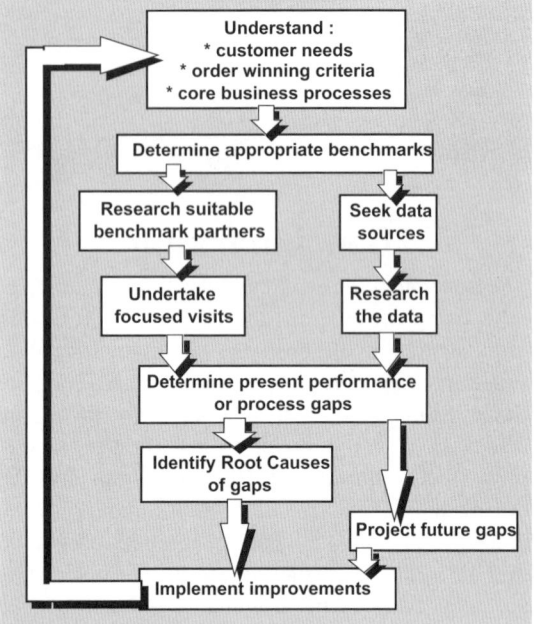

How to measure

Internal benchmark information is relatively easy to obtain. Now comes the external information. There is a huge number of potential sources of benchmark information. But it must be ethically collected and secured (The Benchmarking Centre has a code of conduct including legality, exchange (give and take, not just take), confidentiality (not publishing or passing on ideas to third party competitors), and use.) For competitive benchmarking some possibilities are: a library database search, commercial press cutting databases, specialist industry reviews in newspapers or journals, specialist surveys (e.g. by *The Economist Intelligence Unit*), trade magazines, conference papers and proceedings (managers love to tell of their achievements at such events), market research, special surveys, factory visits and evening meetings of relevant societies, annual financial reports and published accounts, trade and sales literature, quotations from the companies themselves, management consultants and academics (who may be prepared to disclose general information while disguising names). Several authors have made the point that benchmarking is not "industrial tourism" (just visiting), nor is there any point in visiting companies that are in such a totally different league of organisation or technology that there is no chance of catching up.

Many benchmarking exercises will involve actual use of competitor products, including one-way viewing through mirrors of customer usage, and full technical disassembly.

Using benchmarks

Benchmarking is not static. It aims at projecting future trends. So when the internal and external benchmarks are assembled, analysts can begin to assess the critical question of whether the "gap" between own and competitor performance is widening or narrowing. This leads to the establishment of areas for priority action. Competitive benchmarking can become a management philosophy in itself, with the attempt being to remain or achieve "industry best" position in the particular niches identified as important. As soon as one set of improvements has been implemented, it all begins again. It's the Deming cycle.

Benchmarking Beware!

To quote Womack and Jones in *Lean Thinking*: "to hell with benchmarking!". The only true benchmark is the zero waste operation. And Christensen warns of benchmarking yesterday's advantage. (See the Disruptive Technology section).

Further reading

Robert Camp, *Benchmarking*, ASQ Quality Press, 1989

Gregory Watson, *The Benchmarking Workbook*, Productivity Press, 1992

Robert C. Camp, *Business Process Benchmarking*, ASQ Quality Press, 1995

See www.benchmarking.co.uk and www.apqc.org

Best Demonstrated Practice

Best Demonstrated Practice (BDP) is a form of internal Benchmarking. It assembles the best features of several operations to create a benchmark of a theoretical operation comprising the best features of each. For instance, in an insurance company one branch may have the best life policy service, another branch the best walk-in service, a third the best postal response time. So the best theoretical branch could comprise the best demonstrated practice from each.

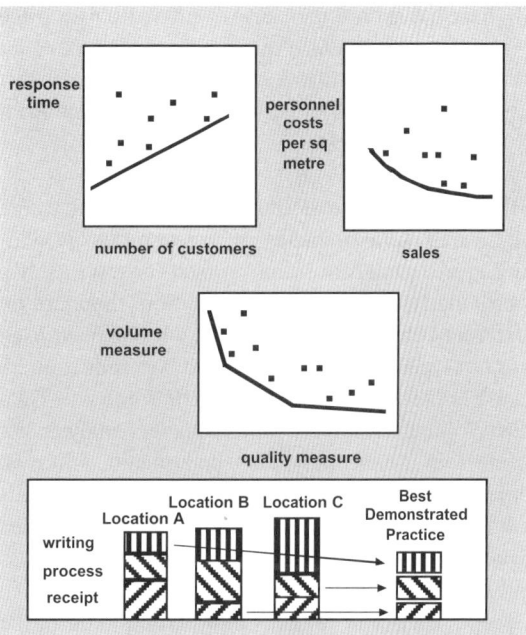

Assuming that an organisation has several similar operations, the steps are as follows :

* Establish the prime measure of interest. For quality, this may be response time or queue time, a customer satisfaction measure, or a defect level, error rate, or number of complaints. For costs the measure could be contribution level, a resource utilisation level, or a comparable cost such as personnel cost per square metre. The measures should be measurable without much controversy. These measures should be carefully chosen, often in association with representative staff from operations, and be related to corporate objectives.

* Establish a suitable measure or measures against which to analyse the prime measure. Examples may be number of customers or products, sales or turnover, or size or area of operation.

* Plot the graph and analyse with branch representatives. Examples are shown. Usually an envelope or lower bound will be formed. This represents the best demonstrated practice. These are the locations to learn from. And operations furthest from the line should get attention: What special problems do they have? What are the causes? After discussion the group may conclude that there are subgroups involved within which it is possible to learn, and that nothing can be learned by comparing some locations with others.

BDP is applicable in decentralised operations where there are several branches, offices or outlets providing approximately the same products or services. It is particularly useful where, in addition, there are no external benchmarks. The approach has been used for both quality improvement and cost reduction. A more sophisticated version of BDP known as Data Envelopment Analysis, which enables analysis beyond two dimensions to be undertaken, relies on linear programming. This mathematical technique is often not warranted because of data uncertainties when an approximation is good enough and has presentational difficulties. The real challenge lies in acceptance of the findings and participation in the analysis, both of which are inhibited by sophisticated mathematics.

BDP can be used in conjunction with several other techniques in this book, such as flowcharting (to better understand the process), SPC (to identify branches that are operating beyond the control limits), and Six Sigma. It should not be used as a "big stick" by management to chase apparent laggards but rather to explore reasons for deviation and opportunities for improvement and learning.

Further reading:
Michael Norman and Barry Stoker, *Data Envelopment Analysis,* Wiley, 1991

Blitz

A Blitz event, also known as "Kaizen Blitz" and Kaikaku, is a short (typically 3 to 5 day) highly focused improvement exercise. Blitz events became hugely popular in the late 1990's in manufacturing and are now beginning to appear in service. A main motivation is the apparently huge productivity gains (20% to 40% not untypical) that can be achieved over a very short period.

The "secret" of such events is the fact that a dedicated team, usually comprising both insiders and outsiders, tackle the focused area full time for a few days, and literally don't take "No" for an answer. "Just do it" is a common phrase – that is, don't write reports, do big analysis, seek permission, but just go for it. Another "secret" is that the events do not seek perfection, just improvement. So you don't "waste time" analysing all the alternatives and carrying out a full financial justification.

Blitz events can concentrate on general improvement or can target specific aims such as quality, 5S, safety, layout, or inventory reduction. Several companies have now held a series of Blitz events in the same area of the plant, but each time coming back with a different emphasis. Remarkable results continue.

Briefly, a typical event may comprise:
* Monday: brief the team, perhaps do some brief education on waste or quality, and plan what will be done. Begin data collection, mapping, investigation.
* Tuesday: Continue investigation. Plan the actual changes. Begin the actual changes.
* Wednesday: Implementation day. Do it. Try it. Do it again. Perhaps 75% of the changes will be in place by day end.
* Thursday: Complete implementation. Verify. Standardise and write standards.
* Friday: Identify and list future opportunities and completion dates for activities that have not been possible during the week, Present. Celebrate.

A quote from Henry Ford seems appropriate to Blitz events: "Whether you believe you can, or whether you believe you can't, you're absolutely right!".

The Blitz team is normally "equipped" with a range of basic tools, such as the "7 tools" and "7 wastes" in this book. Also some basic concepts such as takt time, pull systems, pokayoke are useful.

Choice of team is critical. There must be an experienced facilitator. There must be operators from the area. There must be first line managers from the area. There must be management representation on the team. Very often it is useful to have outsiders, either from other parts of the company or even from outside of the company. You want the "silly" questions to be asked.

Blitz events can be used as part of an ongoing programme of continual improvement. Here they would alternate with other incremental improvement activities such as quality circles, suggestion schemes, mapping, or deliberate inventory withdrawal.

Experience with Blitz events is decidedly mixed. Often dramatic improvements are obtained during the event but sustaining the improvements is another issue. So many have been delighted in the short term, but disappointed in the long term. However experience is now building. The following seem critical:

* Careful choice of area – preferably some form of process mapping to identify areas of opportunity.
* Good briefing of management, including that detailed permission to make changes will not be sought during the event, a realistic idea of what to expect, and management support and enthusiasm both at the end of the event and continuing.
* Having support groups (Maintenance, Quality, possibly Logistics) on standby during the event so that air lines, power points, some machines, stillages, can be moved.)
* Management participation on the team
* A very careful coaching, briefing, training of first line managers. The impact of a Blitz event must be thought through. If you were a first line manager from an area, and here comes some "smart ass" who makes a 30% improvement in your area in 5 days – what would you think, and would you support its sustainability? On this, it used to be thought that Blitz events were 80% technical; we now realise that 80% of time needs to be spent on preparation.
* A big emphasis on standardisation ("holding the gains") towards the end of the event. Standard operating procedures should be written by people from the area itself.
* Clear responsibility for follow-up actions. Some events schedule specific follow up dates.
* Ensuring continuing management interest.

(See the separate section on Sustainability.)

Blitz events can also be used for training. Here the week is spent alternating between short lecture topics and immediate practical exercises applying the material immediately. Here the event ends with a "showcase", not a presentation. These events take much more preparation.

Further reading:
John Bicheno, *STORMFLOW, A kaikaku kit,* PICSIE Books, 2000
Anthony Laraia, Patricia Moody, Robert Hall, *The Kaizen Blitz: Accelerating Breakthroughs in Productivity and Performance*, Wiley, New York, 1999

The best magazine with regular reports on Blitz events is *Target* (the periodical of the Association for Manufacturing Excellence – AME).
Web site: www.ame.org

Better Brainstorming

Brainstorming is a vastly popular technique for idea generation. But beware!

Although a popular technique, research shows brainstorming to yield results that are often worse than obtained by the same number of individuals working alone. The Nominal Group Technique (NGT) is often superior – see the separate section on this. Yet brainstorming may still be worthwhile to do to focus the team on a common problem, to build up team spirit, and to improve communication. A mixed strategy is probably best – use brainstorming for some general aspects, but individual creativity for specialised aspects. Also use brainstorming in series – breaking an overall problem down into elements, and sequencing sessions appropriately. Certainly if brainstorming is used casually without planning, it can be a poor technique.

Several "rules of thumb" have been established for a good brainstorming session. These are

* The group size should be approximately 5 to 9
* Quantity rather than quality of ideas is emphasised; evaluation comes later
* No judgement or criticism is allowed.
* Participants should be stimulated by the ideas of others. This means they have to listen and develop.
* All ideas should be noted down. You may make use of a fishbone diagram
* No hierarchy. All ideas carry equal status. No person should dominate.
* The facilitator or recorder should not allow discussion, lengthy explanation or criticism.
* Humour and "way-out" ideas are encouraged. Having fun works.
* The final stage is grouping of ideas, perhaps using "affiliation diagrams" (see separate section)

The problems with brainstorming have been summarised by Furnham as

* "Social loafing" where a few participants exert less effort and allow others to carry the load. Apparently this is strongly influenced by the perceptions of the participants as to eventual use and importance, and their position.
* "Evaluation apprehension" where participation is influenced by the fear of looking foolish or of being criticised.
* "Production blocking" where ideas that are coming thick and fast have to queue up and are forgotten or are considered less relevant.

A good facilitator should be aware of these, and give gentle encouragement.

Furnham suggests that "Electronic Brainstorming" is far more effective, Here participants work independently via a computer but have access to the developing ideas of others. These have several benefits including shorter meetings, more and better ideas, easier to set up, better documentation, and cost savings.

Further reading
Adrian Furnham, "The Brainstorming Myth", *Business Strategy Review*, Vol 11 No 4, Winter 2000, pp 21-28
Weatherall and J Nunamaker, *Introduction to Electronic Meetings*, Technical Graphics, Chichester, 1996

Cost of Quality (CoQ)

Cost of quality aims at the financial quantification of all activities involved in the prevention, inspection and rectification of defects. The idea is that if the locations and magnitudes of quality related costs are measured and brought to the attention of management, this will be a powerful force for directed improvement. Cost of quality analysis may range from one-off estimates to a complete parallel accounting system. Traditionally, quality is measured by a series of ratios. The problem is that these are seldom comprehensive and lack common units. Ratios should be supplemented by costs, which should be publicised throughout the organization. CoQ can provide specific cost justification data for a management pondering the question of quality "hype" against quality benefit.

If your organization is considering implementing Cost of Quality in a comprehensive way, it would be advisable to obtain the British Standard (BS 6143) "Guide to the economics of quality prevention", or the various guides published by the American Society for Quality. What follows are some general principles.

The conventional quality costing categories are:

* **prevention costs** : the costs of measures to prevent defects from taking place. This would include training, "pokayoke" (see Shingo), and capability studies and improvement (see SPC).
* **appraisal costs** : costs incurred in the detection of defects. This would include testing and inspection.
* **internal failure costs** : all failure costs incurred by internal customers. The costs incurred to rectify defects and failures internally, before the product or service reaches an external customer. This includes costs of scrap, rework, and all internal activities incurred through "not getting it right first time".
* **external failure costs** : all failure costs incurred by external customers. The costs incurred to rectify products and services after they have reached external customers, including returns, warranty claims, complaints, field repair, and perhaps lost custom.

Phil Crosby groups the first two, referring to them as "POC" (price of conformance), and the second two as "PONC" (price of nonconformance). For simplicity we can refer to the first two as "prevention costs" and the second two as "failure costs".

Traditionally, prevention and failure costs have been seen as a trade-off. Total costs are the sum of failure costs and prevention and appraisal costs. As quality levels improve, failure costs decline. However, there is some controversy about the rate at which prevention and appraisal costs need to rise to keep failure costs falling. Traditionalists say that prevention and appraisal costs have to rise exponentially. This means there is a quality level beyond which it simply does not pay to go on improving. Total quality advocates say that as quality becomes the way of life, although prevention and appraisal costs continue to rise this rise will be less than the rate at which failure costs are falling. In this case the optimal quality cost level is perfection.

Whatever. The proven Cost of Quality view is that prevention pays. Putting effort into prevention will more than pay for itself by a reduction in appraisal costs, but mostly by a big reduction in failure costs both internal and external. This is shown in the figure. This figure is central to quality management.

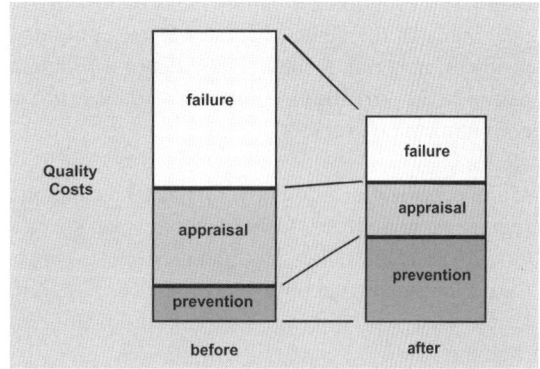

The point is that cost of quality analysis does set out to quantify what poor quality actually costs. The results, in many organizations that have implemented CoQ, are often "shock treatment". The cost of not getting it right first time is typically in the range of 20% to 25% of turnover. So the savings that can be achieved by improving quality are very large, and the associated investment often more cost effective than the costs of increasing turnover - including marketing and capacity acquisition.

CoQ pinpoints the sources of quality costs. It is a Pareto view - identify the big sources of quality costs and hit them first. Specific budgets can then be set and controlled. Juran, the early pioneer of cost of quality, sees CoQ as an essential feature of his "trilogy" (see the section on Juran). So quality becomes a closely managed function, using money (the "language of management" according to Juran), rather than having quality as something that is desirable and "nice" but, when it comes to the point, really of low priority.

Some more advanced CoQ systems now incorporate cross coding, so that some of the costs that are booked into the normal costing system are cross linked to appropriate CoQ categories. This is not an exact science, and many of the problems that bedevil cost accounting (such as the appropriate allocation of overheads) are to be found in CoQ also. But exactness is not the issue, it is the trends, approximate magnitude, and locations that are important. When setting up these parallel costing systems it is useful to go further than just prevention and failure costs by identifying the source of the defect; operator error, equipment problem, material problem, specification problem, procedural problem, supplier problem or communication problem.

Many organizations do not yet undertake CoQ on a regular ongoing basis. Instead they rely on specific CoQ assessment studies. Here detailed questioning is the norm, usually making use of the process diagram, Pareto analysis, Ishikawa diagram, and histogram. (See the 7 tools.)

CoQ can be seen as closely related to the "7 Wastes". The real aim is not merely to keep on reducing the costs of (poor) quality but to go on reducing the costs of all wastes. Defects are but one of the seven wastes. Some companies have now begun to cost more wastes, either directly or through cost accounting systems such as "activity based costing" (ABC).

Further reading
BS 6143 (Part 2, 1990 and Part 1, 1991), British Standards Institution.
Jack Campanella (ed), *Principles of Quality Costs* (Third edition), ASQ Quality Press, Milwaukee, 1999

Cusum Charts

A "Cusum" or Cumulative Sum Chart is a type of control chart which is particularly useful for detecting small but significant changes in the process. Take a look at the conventional control chart shown and the corresponding cusum chart. Notice that the change is almost undetectable in the control chart, but is very clear on the cusum chart. A large change, on the other hand, is easy to detect on a conventional control chart.

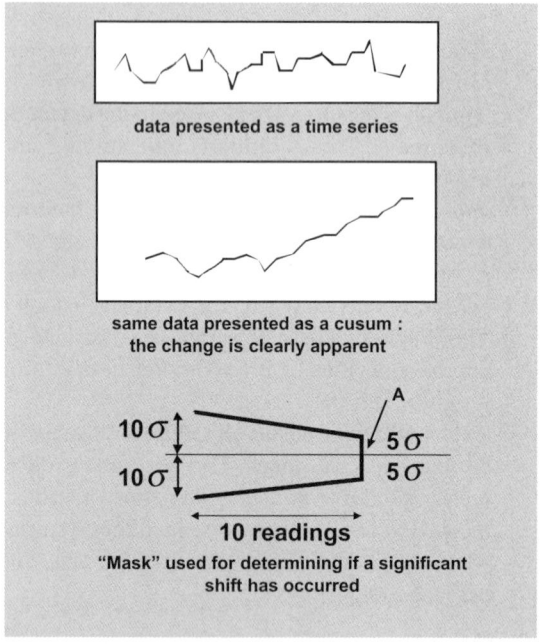

Any situation where it is desirable to detect a sudden change quickly is a candidate for a cusum. Examples are customer enquiries, fuel consumption (cusums are an excellent indicator that something has gone wrong with a vehicle), yield from a chemical process, response times or failure rates.

To plot a cusum, merely subtract the average (or target) value of the process from the actual measurement, add the resulting number to the previously accumulated number and plot it on the chart. It will be appreciated that if the average remains unchanged the resulting cusum will hover around a constant value, but if the average changes the graph will "take off" either up or down.

With conventional control charts, control limits are needed to detect if a real change has taken place. With a cusum, a "V Mask" is used. To construct a V Mask you need to calculate the standard deviation of the process measurements. This will require a minimum of 20 readings. Then draw the V Mask as shown in the figure on a transparent sheet. Lay the V Mask with point A (the head) over the latest reading, keeping the mask horizontal. A change is significant if the cusum line crosses one of the trailing arms.

Further reading

BS5703, *Guide to Data Analysis and Quality Control using Cusums*, Parts 1 to 4, British Standards Institution, Milton Keynes, 1982

J. Murdich, *Control Charts*, Macmillan, London, 1979

Data Display

Radar Charts

Also known as a web chart or a glyph chart, this type of chart is useful for the display of several performance indicators simultaneously. Deterioration in performance and relative speed of moving towards a goal is easily seen. Some companies display these charts prominently for all employees to see. In a radar chart, the target is at the centre, and the starting position shown near the circumference. Measures are plotted on lines joining the circumference to the centre: the closer to the centre, the better. At Unipart UK these charts are known as "Ten D to Zero" meaning that the target is zero (perfection, at the bullseye) and the starting point is 10.

To draw a radar chart:
1. Decide on the number of measures to be charted. Split these into two groups: those where more is better and those where less is better. These two types of measures are shown above and below the centreline. Further grouping may be desired; for instance, all quality measures together, and all people measures together.
2. Decide the targets, and the present positions of each of the measures. The target values should be shown at the centre. Choose a suitable scale for each measure, with the present situation shown some two-thirds along each line.
3. Arrange the spacing of the measure arms to be uniformly spread. (The angle between measures should be 360 degrees divided by the number of measures in each group + 1).
4. Plot the current status of the measures at regular intervals. Join the plots to form the web.

A sample chart is shown in the figure.

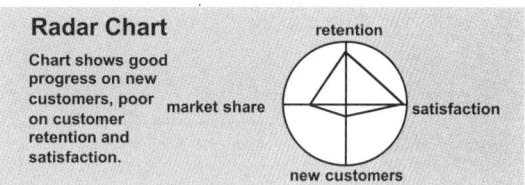

Box and Whisker Diagrams, and Numbered Histograms

Variability is important in quality. To quote Ishikawa, "data without variability is false data". Deming agrees, claiming that most managers have very poor understanding of variation and make poor decisions as a result. So this section gives some practical easy ways to show variation.

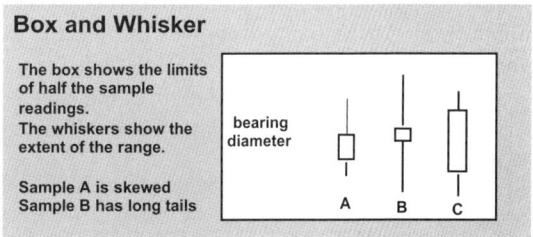

Box and whisker diagrams are a clear way to show variation on a control chart. Say you have taken a sample of 20 readings. Arrange the readings in ascending order. The box shows the range of the middle 10 readings, and the whiskers show the range of all 20 readings. In other words, the box shows the limits of the first and third quartiles, and the whiskers the minimum and maximum values. Within the box, a line is drawn to indicate the median (i.e. the middle value in a set of readings arranged from lowest to highest). (Where the sample is large, the whiskers may show the extent of 97.5% of the readings, with individual readings beyond this range shown as dots.) Such diagrams are an instant way to appreciate the spread of data; particularly where the data is skewed (i.e. not evenly spread around the median value).

The numbered histogram uses the actual readings to fill in the bars of the histogram. In this way, a reader can get the actual numbers if she wishes or merely gain an overall impression from the bars. Examples are shown in the figure.

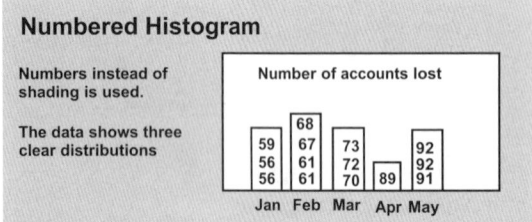

Manhattan Diagrams

Manhattan Diagrams are a form of stacked bar chart. These can be a very efficient way of showing trends within trends and multiple-dimension quality data.

Take a cricket example. Hour by hour the stacked chart shows total runs made and who was responsible for the runs. Alternatively the bowler responsible for the runs. In a hotel or a plant, total defects for the week are shown by the overall length of bar, and the categories of defect or complaint shown within the bar.

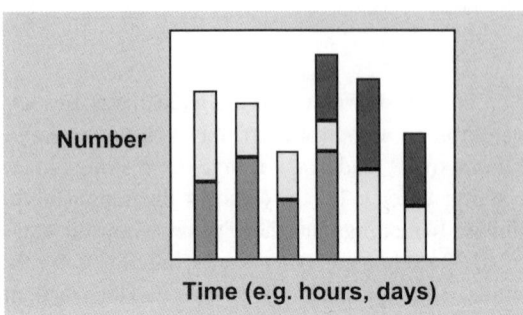

Defects per Million Opportunities (DPMO)

Defects per million opportunities (DPMO) is a quality metric that allows for product or service complexity. It has become closely associated with Six Sigma. So, for instance, comparing defect rates per unit for two printed circuit boards that differ markedly on the number of components may not be meaningful, but using DPMO allows benchmarking both internally and sometimes externally. It allows month to month comparisons irrespective of product mix.

Recording end of line defects is often not satisfactory. There may be a significant amount of rework along the line resulting in a very low final defect rate for the completed product. (In fact, this is a ruse adopted by some Japanese companies' world class quality performance). But this would be self-delusion. Moreover, the actual sources of the defects might be missed or not recorded.

Conceptually DPMO is a great idea. But "opportunities" are difficult to pin down. Motorola had a DPMO committee to standardise the approach. Here we will consider two examples.

A printed circuit board has 1 board, 119 components, 56 solder joints, and 2 glue points. The board must be cut, printed, and cleaned. There are therefore $3 + 119 + 56 + 2 = 180$ defect opportunities per board. Sometimes this is referred to as OFD – opportunities for defects. Notice that inspection defects are not included. Also notice that the company could also record the defects per million components (DPMC = component defects x 1m / 119) or defects per million joints (DPMJ = joint defects x 1m / 56). The DPMO is then (total defects x 1000000) / (OFD x number of boards).

A hotel decides that to get to a DPMO figure they will trace a typical guest visit. This involves check in, checkout, and room and breakfast experience each day. The management decides to group all possible check in errors into three "opportunities" – data, accounts and other. Room opportunities are grouped into bedroom and bathroom. Breakfast is one opportunity. During an average overnight stay the hotel decides to allocate one opportunity for bar, restaurant, room service and other possibilities. The hotel therefore records complaints under each of these categories and sets the OFD opportunities using the formula 4 + 4 x (no of nights stay) per guest visit. Notice in this case that it might be argued that there are many more defect opportunities – for instance each keystroke entering data at the front desk. But this would be to overcomplicate matters – one data entry error is recorded however many mistakes are made. Also notice that defects are not necessarily complaints – a failure to meet own internal standards is also recorded as a defect. The DPMO is (total complaints or errors x 1000000) / (guests x 3 + guest nights x 4).

In some manufacturing business, for example electronics, DPMO data can be used as a design aid. For instance if the rate of joint defects is high, designers will try to reduce the number of joints in future designs.

There is also a possible link between DPMO and CoQ (Cost of Quality – see separate section). In the examples above it will be realised that not all the defect categories or opportunities are likely to involve the same cost to the organisation. So an additional refinement is to weight the various opportunity categories by a dollar amount. These dollar amounts would not be actual costs, but would give an indication of the cost of poor quality. This is a very neat way to bring failure to the attention of management.

In Six Sigma studies it is not only the single DPMO figure that is important, but also the distribution. So the board manufacturer and hotel may wish to record weekly data and plot the distribution over the last quarter. A narrow distribution is better than a spread out distribution because it indicates less variation. The "ultimate" Six Sigma goal is nominally 3.4 DPMO, but it can be seen through the examples above that 4 sigma (6200 DPMO) or 5 sigma (620 DPMO) may well be very challenging.

Design of Experiments

Design of Experiments (DOE) is a family of techniques, which enables a quality professional to home in rapidly on the most important variables in new product design or process improvement. DOE has a long history going back to Sir Ronald Fisher in 1930, but popularised by Taguchi and Box. Six Sigma has given DOE a big boost. Shainin techniques are related.

There is a classic exercise in quality that involves the use of a catapult. A ball is fired and the length of flight measured. The first task is to standardise the process to ensure that variation is minimised. Then one can begin to determine the set of variables or FACTORS (to use the DOE term) that results in the longest throw. Some factors are the type of ball, the pull-back firing angle, the angle of the base, length of elastic, the position of the ball holder, the position of the top pin, and the position of the bottom pin. If each of these 7 factors had just two settings (or LEVELS in DOE speak) there would be $2^7 = 128$ possibilities. It is just possible to try out all 128, firing 2 or 3 balls (called an OBSERVATION) for each setting (or TREATMENT). This is called FULL FACTORIAL. But for more factors or more levels this becomes impractical. DOE offers the solution. An orthogonal array, available from tables, is chosen which allows a drastic reduction in the number of observations necessary. Generally full factorials are the better choice where taking observations is low cost and not disruptive, but this is not often the case.

Treatments	Factors Levels			Observations (cm.)	
	Ball	Angle	Elastic		
1	-1	-1	-1	190	210
2	-1	+1	+1	210	215
3	+1	-1	+1	210	220
4	+1	+1	-1	225	240

- Notice that each column has the same number of levels, denoted by +1 and -1
- -1 denotes a small ball, narrow angle, short elastic, +1 denotes big, wide, long
- The same array can be used for 2 or 3 factors

Take the example shown in the figure. Here there are three factors say ball, angle and elastic and two levels for each. Plus indicates 'big' and minus 'small'. Notice the orthogonal array requires only four treatments of two observations each. There is an equal number of + and – signs in each column. The observations in cm. are recorded with reference to some datum. Notice the symmetry of the calculations. Apparently the best setting occurs with treatment 2 which is for small ball, large angle, long elastic.

Treatments	Factors			Observations (cm.)	
	A	B	C		
1	-1	-1	-1	-20	0
2	-1	+1	+1	0	5
3	+1	-1	+1	0	10
4	+1	+1	-1	15	20

For A, level -1; (-20+0+0+5)/4 = -3.75
For A, level +1; (0+10+15+20)/4 = 13.75
For B, level -1; (-20+0+0+10)/4 =
For B, level +1; (0+5+15+20)/4 =
For C, level -1; =
For C, level +1; =

One can investigate further, What if there are 'interaction effects', like ball being affected by angle. An interaction effect table can be drawn up as shown showing the effect of angle on ball, angle on elastic, and elastic on ball. An observation is taken for each possibility. An interaction plot can be drawn for each pair, as shown. If the lines cross there is interaction, which would indicate more care is required, but if not you have a more robust solution.

An industrial example may be to identify the critical and non-critical factors for tile making. This is extremely valuable since monitoring, energy and sometimes material costs can be reduced. In practice the relevant factors are obtained through experience or group brainstorming. Software is available which can guide non-statisticians to a good solution provided that they maintain common sense such as taking valid observations at random intervals.

There is no doubt that DOE is essential to achieving world class levels of quality in manufacturing such as the Six Sigma programme. For improvement, DOE is an order of magnitude more powerful than the basic 7 tools.

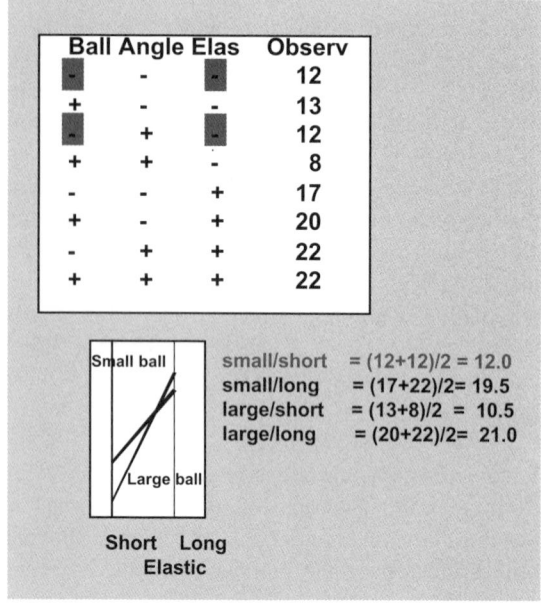

Despite considerable support, not all companies have achieved success through the Taguchi approach. It is still quite complex for the non statistician. More recently, Dorian Shainin has further refined and simplified DOE. His methods involve even more "engineering judgement" than those of Taguchi, and are not accepted by all purists. An additional problem is that the Shainin methods have in general not been written up to the extent of Taguchi, and are also subject to copyright. Nevertheless the Shainin techniques deserve considerably more attention than they have been given.

Further Reading:
Keki R Bhote and Adi Bhote, *World Class Quality*, Second Edition, AmaCom, 2000. Reviews traditional DOE and gives a full explanation of Shainin DOE.
Glen Stuart Peace, *Taguchi Methods : A Hands-On Approach*, Addison Wesley, 1993. A very comprehensive treatment of Taguchi.
Larry B Barrentine, *An Introduction to Design of Experiments : A Simplified Approach*. ASQ Quality Press, Milwaukee, 1999. An easy-to-understand introduction - sufficient for most purposes

Disruptive Technologies

Two of the primary rules in quality management are listen to your customers, and continuously improve. Also, benchmark! Are there situations in which this is not only misguided but also deadly? Perhaps so – where there are so called Disruptive Technologies at work.

Clayton Christensen of Harvard has produced a brilliant and seminal analysis. Christensen distinguishes "sustaining technologies" from "disruptive technologies". A disruptive technology is one that classically starts small, is simpler than the existing technology, and is ignored or even scorned at early stages by customers and managers alike. But the technology develops until suddenly it becomes a serious proposition. Customers "don't know that they want it until they want it". Meanwhile the sustaining or established technology continues to improve, often outstripping the needs of many customers. There is the danger that companies compete by continuous improvement, often putting their best people on this, but ignoring the challenge of the new approach. Witness vacuum cleaners and Dyson.

Improvement can create a void that the typically low cost disruptive technology fills. Customers think they want it, but don't know about the alternatives. By then it is often too late for companies with the sustaining technology to catch up. Witness Amazon.com as against established booksellers who offered sofas and coffee. Other examples are mini computers displacing mainframes, and eventually being displaced themselves by networked PCs. Or department stores being displaced by discounters. Or Visa and MasterCard displacing Sears' dominant store card. Note here that "technology" refers to a concept rather than a physical technology.

Christensen states that with a disruptive technology many of the normal rules of business don't apply. Thus market research, allocating resources, killing off low return business, investment hurdles, and continuous improvement are all good policy for sustaining technologies, but may be the very policies that prove deadly in the presence of a disruptive technology. "Markets that don't exist can't be analysed". This is not a failure of poor management; it is the very fact that they have done everything right that causes them to fail. The "innovator's dilemma" is that continuing innovation, listening to customers and going after more lucrative developments is precisely wrong.

Precisely because a disruptive technology displays minimal initial impact on corporate growth or exiting markets it fails to attract the interest of executives who must look for far bigger gains. Christensen suggests that the way to deal with disruptive technologies is to establish a completely separate division, perhaps geographically separated but certainly organisationally separated from the parent, where small innovations are still viewed with excitement. This happened in the successful start-up of IBM's PC division or HP's inkjet printer division. Christensen suggests that the management of disruptive technologies requires different resources, different processes, and different values to those required for sustaining technologies. Strong visionary leadership is required, but also a different sort of leader to those skilled at managing sustaining business. Reading Christensen's brilliant analysis leaves the open question, "Is that why so many kaizen or lean initiatives fail to deliver?" (Because the mindset is about sustainability, not radical change.)

Christensen points out that imitation is sometimes precisely the wrong thing to do. It may build only yesterday's competitive advantage. Successful strategies need to have a deep understanding of the processes of developing competition, not the transient 'solutions'.

Further reading
Clayton Christensen, *The Innovator's Dilemma: When New Technologies Cause Great Firms to Fail*, Harvard Business School Press, 1997
Clayton Christensen, "The Past and Future of Competitive Advantage", *MIT Sloan Management Review*, Winter 2001, pp 105-109

Failure Modes and Effect Analysis (FMEA)

Failure mode and effect analysis (FMEA) is a methodology to assess and reduce risk in systems, products or services. It aims to define, identify, prioritise, and eliminate known or potential failures at an early a stage as possible. FMEA is a Pareto type of analysis, homing in on the "vital few" failure modes. It is often used in conjunction with QFD (see separate section). As QFD is deployed from stage to stage, a corresponding FMEA is carried out. Other techniques used with FMEA include flowcharting, cause and effect diagrams, brainstorming / nominal group technique, process capability (Cpk) and design of experiments (see separate sections). The SERVQUAL dimensions are useful in service FMEA. With increasing risk of litigation in connection with products and services, several large companies (eg. Ford) require their suppliers to undertake FMEA analyses. But whether the aim is reduced risk from litigation or improved customer satisfaction, FMEA is becoming a standard procedure to be applied to all new products and services.

FMEA usually begins by assembling a group who are familiar with the product, service or system. If possible the group should include customers (internal or external), marketing and field service. The group will have the task of brainstorming out all the possible causes of failure. In addition to brainstorming, designers and engineers will be able to advise on likely modes of failure and records may show failures in past performance.

The four types of FMEA form a hierarchy, and can be used independently or in sequence. A System FMEA is used at the design stage to analyse overall systems including the interactions between functions so as to minimise failure effects. A Design FMEA is used to minimise design faults before they are passed to manufacturing. The Process FMEA focuses on failures caused in the manufacturing process. Service FMEA focuses on service failures. All four FMEAs use basically the same procedure and analysis sheet, an example of which is shown in the figure.

The first stage is to obtain a sketch or engineering drawing of the system, product or service. Then a flowchart (process chart) of the product or service should be drawn up. Then, using the flowchart, step by step, all possible failure modes should be written down. The team should ask itself how could the process fail, and what might be found unacceptable by the customer. If warranty, field failure, or customer complaints data is available for a similar product or service this should be used. In a process or design FMEA the team should consider, for each step of the chart or component on the drawing, the inputs (parts, supply, testing), the process (manufacture), and outputs (inspection, transport, storage).

Failures		Rankings			Risk Priority Number (RPN)
potential mode of failure	potential causes and effects of failure	Severity (A)	Occurrence	Detection (C)	
		1 = none	1 = never	1 = certain	
		3 = slight	3 = v slight	3 = high	
		5 = moderate	5 = low	5 = medium	(A) * (B) * (C)
		7 = major	7 = mod high	7 = slight	
		9 = serious	9 = v high	9 = remote	
		10 = hazard	10 = almost certain	10 = almost impossible	

The effects of each mode of failure is then analysed under three criteria - severity, occurrence, and detection. (This is easy to remember: the mnemonic for the three criteria is SOD. FMEA tries to get to the root of the failure. Around roots are sods of earth.) For each mode of failure, the group allocates a score for each of the three. A 10 point scale is recommended. Severity indicates the seriousness of a failure, viewed from the perspective of the system or the customer. Occurrence is a rating reflecting the estimated number (or frequency) of failure. Detection reflects the possibility that a fault or problem will be discovered before it is released to the next stage (for system or design FMEAs) or to the final customer (manufacturing or service FMEAs). Like several other techniques much of the benefit of FMEA is derived from the discussions amongst group members as they assign relative scores. Thereafter the "RPN" or risk priority number is calculated by multiplying the three factors (S x O x D).

When all failure modes have been considered, the most critical or highest priority modes are identified by ranking the RPN scores. Clearly a high score indicates reasonable severity, more likely to occur, with reasonable difficulty of detection. Of course suitable actions must now be taken, in priority order. A threshold is usually established, above which action must be taken. For a 10 point scale the maximum RPN score is 1000 points, but the threshold may be as low as an RPN of 10 or 20. Once the threshold RPN number has been decided, the team should assess all modes of failure above the threshold for risk. If risk is small, no action is needed, but if high, action becomes essential.

Further reading:
D.H. Stamatis, *Failure Mode and Effect Analysis*, ASQ Quality Press, Milwaukee, WI, 1995

Force Field Analysis

The force field diagram is a simple but very effective tool to identify, in good time, the various "pressures" for and against change. A force field diagram is typically used early on in the implementation of quality programs such as SPC, may also be used for introducing change on a much smaller scale. Force field diagrams were introduced by an organizational analyst, Kurt Lewin, in the 1920s. Their beauty lies in their simplicity which enables any employee to grasp and use the concept in minutes.

Consider a change, any change, that is being introduced within the organization. This may be an attempt to reduce defects or improve service. The concept is simply that a chart is put up with a vertical line drawn on it. This represents the "status quo", or position at present. To the left of the line are listed the forces encouraging change to take place. To the right are the forces resisting the change. The pressures for change oppose the forces resisting change. In a service delivery case, where speed of delivery is the problem, the forces for change could include customer expectations. Staff fears over redundancy may be opposing the change. Whether change will actually come about is dependent upon whether the forces for change will become dominant. To identify the forces at an early stage is half the battle - the forces for change can be effectively utilized and the forces opposing change effectively tackled. That's it!

An extension of the basic force field diagram is to show the linkages between the opposing forces. An example is shown in the figure.

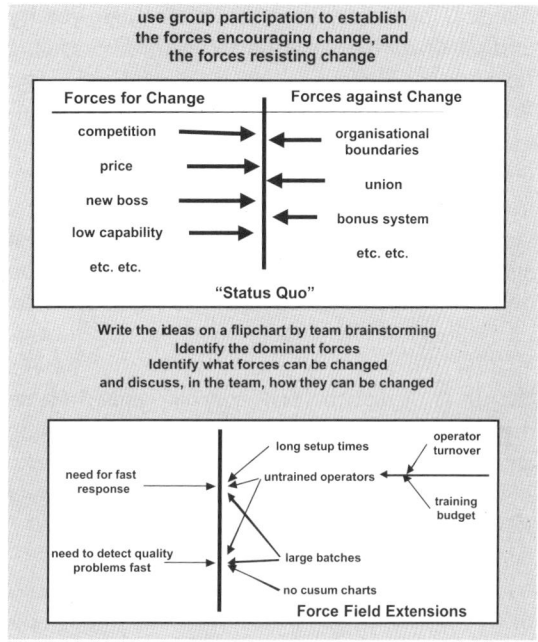

The "trick" of using force field analysis is group participation and brainstorming. Not only does a group think of many factors which an individual would not, but the results become "their" analysis of the problem. Get the people concerned together and ask them, "What are the factors that are tending to push us to make this change?" Enter them on the diagram. Then ask, "OK, now let's think about the factors that are preventing us from making this change." Enter them too. Now ask "What can be done about these factors?". There are two sets of answers: encourage the 'good' forces and reduce the 'bad' forces. This should lead to a set of actions that the group has developed themselves, which can then be tackled. Force field analysis can be used in conjunction with several other techniques and tools. A common one is the cause and effect diagram, which can be used to explore alternatives to the barriers that have been identified.

Hoshin

Hoshin (or Hoshin Kanri but also known as Jishu Kanri and in the West as Policy Deployment, and translated from the Japanese as a "methodology for setting strategic direction"), has become a well-accepted way of planning and communicating quality and productivity goals throughout an organisation. It is the emerging method of **strategic quality and productivity planning** and is used by leading Japanese companies (Toyota, Sony) and by leading Western companies (Hewlett Packard, Texas Instruments, Proctor and Gamble). Juran has pointed out that the concept follows closely the approach long used in managing company finance. It is, in essence, very simple but requires high levels of commitment and time. The objective is to communicate common objectives and gain commitment throughout the organisation.

Hoshin is in fact the PDCA cycle applied on an organisational level. Witcher and Butterworth talk about the FAIR model beginning with the Act stage. Focus (act), Alignment (plan), Integration (do), and Responsiveness (check).

A "Hoshin" is a word that is increasingly being heard in Western companies, to mean the breakthroughs or goals that are required to be achieved so as to meet the overall plan. Thus "what are your hoshins ?" means what are the vital few things that you need to focus on. At the top level there may be only 3 to 5 hoshins. But at lower levels, the hoshins form a network or hierarchy of activities which lead to the top level hoshins. They are developed by consultation. Hoshin objectives are customer focused, based on company wide information, and measurable.

In essence, according to Juran, there are 5 stages :
* the business plan is expanded to include quality and productivity goals, not merely profitability and ROI.
* these goals are deployed down the organisation to determine the required resources, to agree on the actions, and to fix responsibilities
* appropriate measures are developed
* managers review progress regularly
* the reward system is adjusted to support the quality and productivity plan

Hoshin starts with the concept of homing in on the "vital few". Where there is little change in operating conditions, a company still needs to rely upon departmental management, but top management planning is not required. However, where there is significant change, top management must step in and steer the organisation. This requires strategic planning (for future alignment to identify the vital few strategic gaps), strategy management (for change), and cross functional management (to manage horizontal business processes). Hoshin is, however, not a planning tool but an execution tool. It deploys the "voice of the customer", not just the profit goals.

Departmental management should be relied upon for "kaizen" (i.e. incremental) improvements, but breakthrough improvements which often involve cross functional activities and top level support, should be the focus for hoshin planning. (We can note here similarities with related fields - Juran talks about the need for project by project improvement to achieve breakthroughs which attack chronic wastes, in BPR Davenport talks about "sequential alteration" between continuous improvement and process reengineering, and in *Lean Thinking* Womack and Jones discuss kaizen and kaikaku.)

Once the vital few strategic gaps have been identified by top management, employees and teams at each level are required to develop plans as to how to close the gaps. This requires that employees have access to adequate up-to-date information - breaking down "confidentiality" barriers found in many Western organisations. There must be a clear link, or cause and effect relationship, between the organisational goals, key objectives, and activities. Measures, including check points, are developed by the employees themselves. At each level, Deming's Plan, Do, Check, Adjust cycle operates. And, there is strong use of both the "7 tools" and the New Tools (see separate sections) to analyse, quantify, and control. Further, root cause analysis, using the 5 Whys method (see separate section), is used at each level.
The Hoshin concept can be seen as two stages :

Planning for Focus and Planning for Achievement. In the Focus stage, thinking about the 3 to 5 year plan leads to identification of critical success factors and the "vital few" upon which to concentrate. Then in the Achievement stage, breakthrough goals are developed for the vital few areas, which are expanded out into annual targets, which in turn lead to the necessary projects and actions. Top management should be concerned with developing the "vision". But, unlike many western companies, this vision is translated into required actions. One way is to use "backward planning" - starting with the ideal design and working backwards, year by year, to identify the constraints that need to be eliminated.

Hoshin Process

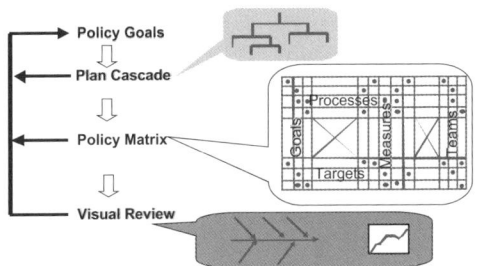

Adapted from Unipart and Oakland *TQM*

Hoshin uses the "outcome, what, how, how much, and who" framework. A Policy Matrix is useful here. At Board level, a visioning process covers the key questions of what is to be the required outcome for the company (e.g. 10% growth), what is to be achieved (e.g. reductions in lead time), how is it to be done (e.g. extend lean manufacturing principles), and how much (all shops to be on JIT by year end). Specific quality and productivity goals are established. Then, the "who" are discussed. Normally there will be several managers responsible for achieving these objectives. Appropriate measures are also developed.

The Hoshin plans are cascaded in a Tree Diagram form. This cascading process is also different to most traditional models. In traditional models, cascading plans come down from the top without consultation, and there is little vertical and especially horizontal alignment. In Hoshin, people who must implement the plan design the plan. The means, not just the outcomes, must be specified. And there are specific and ongoing checks to see that local plans add up to overall plans. The matrix is used to assure horizontal alignment.

At each level a group meeting takes place. This is referred to as "Catch Ball" (ideas are tossed around like a ball) or "Huddles". Ideas flow from all directions, and agreement is arrived at by consensus and negotiation, not authority. If a goal is really infeasible the upper tier is informed. A Japanese word for this is the "Ringi" system.

Feedback goes in the reverse direction. Difficulties and constraints are identified and fed back to the level above who are required to act accordingly. Also, measures are taken and gaps identified. If a problem is identified, corrective action is taken in relation to the process, not the person. This "blame free" culture is critical.

A final stage in the cycle is the Hoshin Review where achievements against plan are formally rolled up the organisation. This uses visual results where possible. Exceptions are noted and carried forward. Hewlett Packard does this very formally once per quarter, "flagging up" (by yellow or red "flag") problem areas. Intel uses, against each Hoshin, a classification showing highlights, lowlights, issues, and plans. Again, root causes are identified.

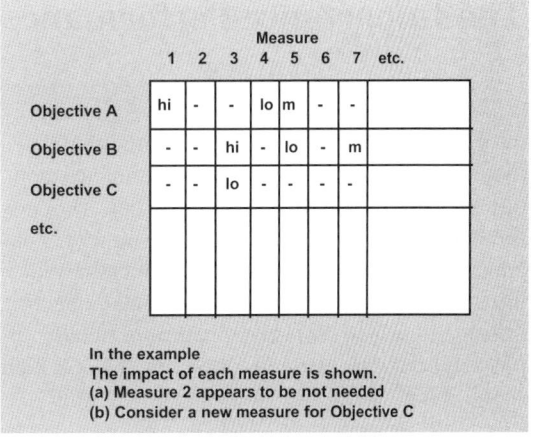

In the example
The impact of each measure is shown.
(a) Measure 2 appears to be not needed
(b) Consider a new measure for Objective C

The tools of Hoshin are similar to QFD and Matrix Analysis. When the objectives have been discussed and clarified they are set down in a matrix against the existing measures, as shown. This enables a review of measures identifying measurement gaps, redundant measures, and excessive measures. "Deployment" man take place using a series of matrices. First, objectives against processes. This identifies the most important processes. Second, processes against measures.

Hoshin is in essence an expanded form of "team briefing" but requires written commitment, identification of goals, the setting of measures, and discussion at each level. In Western companies, top management sometimes spends much time on corporate vision but then fails to put in place a mechanism to translate the vision into deliverables and measures, at each level in the organisation. Hoshin may go some way to explaining why in Japanese companies the decision making process is slower, but implementation is much faster and smoother.

Further reading:
Y. Akao, *Hoshin Kanri : Policy Deployment for Successful TQM*, Productivity Press, Portland, 1991
Michele L Bechtell, *The Management Compass : Steering the Corporation Using Hoshin Planning*, AMA Management Briefing, New York, 1995

The Importance Performance Matrix

When measuring performance or collecting survey information on service quality, it is important that a two-dimensional view be taken: performance along one axis and importance along the other. This was (probably) first suggested by Kotler in 1987, has appeared in several quality-related publications since then, with the latest variant by Slack et al. Collecting information along these two dimensions greatly improves the utility of the information. Thus a high score on performance may mean "overkill" or "achieving target", and a low score on performance may indicate urgent action or simply low priority. Often quality or customer satisfaction surveys reflect only the dimension of satisfaction or performance but ignore the importance to the customer of the factor being surveyed. This can lead to misleading conclusions. It's a simple but powerful idea.

In a customer survey, using for instance a 1 to 5 rating scale, there should always be two scales for each question : one going from excellent to poor (or performed well to performed badly) to cover satisfaction or performance, and the other from important to not important. Then, when plotted on a matrix, the priority clusters become clear. See the figure.

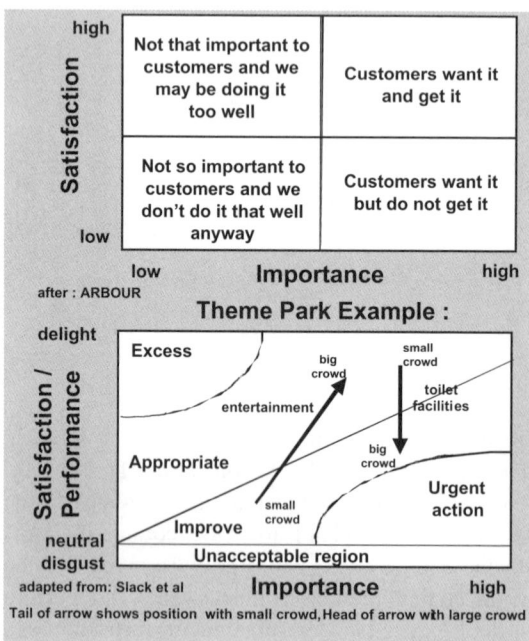

A further dimension is also possible : one could collect the performance importance data by category or market segment and show the variation on a performance importance matrix. For instance, one could categorise performance importance information at a theme park by the number of attendees and discover that some aspects might migrate from the high-low (overkill) quadrant to the low-high (priority) quadrant as the crowd size grows and facilities get pressed for capacity. See the lower figure.

Further reading:
Willard C Hom, "Making Customer Service Analysis a Little Easier with the PGCV Index", *Quality Progress*, Vol 30, No 3, March 1997, pp 89-93
Philip Kotler, *Marketing for Non-profit Organizations*, Prentice Hall, Englewood Cliffs, 1987, pp 635-636
Slack, N., Chambers, Harland, Harrison, Johnston, *Operations Management*, Pitman, London, 1995, p 740.

The Johari Window

The Johari Window (named after its inventors Joe Lufts and Harry Ingham) is useful in fostering clearer understanding and better communication on an interpersonal basis. Teams may also use it. Communication and understanding are of course keys for better quality. The window also helps in building trust.

The idea is that there are things (concepts, facts, assumptions, behaviours etc.) that are known to you and there are things that are not known to you. Likewise there are things known the other person (or team) and things unknown. This leads to a two by two matrix, as shown. The greater the "Arena", and the smaller the other quadrants, the better. To reduce the Blind Spot requires you to solicit feedback from the other person, or the other person to disclose information to you. To reduce the Façade requires either you to give feedback to the other person, or to self disclose formerly unknown information. This has to be done actively. So disclosure and feedback are central characteristics.

Just knowing about the Johari Window helps both sides. Poor communication and knowledge are at the heart of many organisational, quality, and human problems. I always assumed that you had been trained in CNC programming! Did you know that press operator is a model builder whose skills could be of great benefit? Did you know that you have an annoying characteristic of sucking on your teeth that disturbs team concentration? I did not realise that you were nervous about being team leader! So there are obligations to both listen ("seek to understand before seeking to be understood" says Stephen Covey), and to provide appropriate information. Often there is a feedback loop at work – the more you tell me, the more I will tell you, and vice versa. Think in terms of the other person – what would be useful for him to know that I know. Give people the opportunity and time to speak and tell. Ask. Have patience. Don't assume that what you have to say is more important than what others have to say; don't interrupt to add your own (irrelevant?) anecdote. Gently remind others to do the same.

Use the phrase "Remember Johari" whenever necessary.

A variation on the Johari window is to do with attitudes and relationships. Scholtes, for instance, has suggested that the axes are then, "I am OK, I am not OK" and "You are OK, You are not OK". Here the object is get to the Trust quadrant where both sides believe and trust in the other. You are OK, but I am not OK indicates insecurity. If we are both not OK then there is serious mistrust and disruption. If I am OK but you are not, then there is suspicion and "theory Y" type behaviour.

JOHARI WINDOW

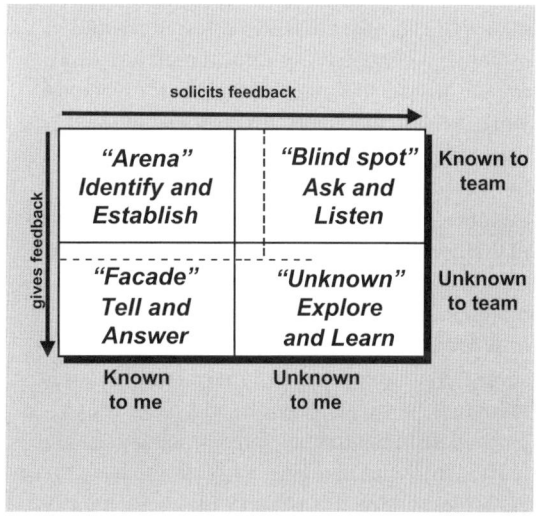

Kaizen

Kaizen is the Japanese name for continuous improvement. As such it is central to Quality and to Lean operations. It brings together several of the tools and techniques described in this book plus a few besides. The word originates from Maasaki Imai who wrote a book of the same name and made Kaizen popular in the West. Although a registered name of the Kaizen Institute, the word is now widely used and understood and has appeared in the English dictionary.

Kaizen can be thought of a series of incremental improvement projects. But a better thought is simply doing better today than yesterday. In a true Kaizen company everyone dedicates to doing this every day.

According to Imai, Kaizen comprises several elements. Kaizen is both a philosophy and a set of tools.

The Philosophy of Kaizen: Quality begins with the customer. But customers' views are continuously changing and standards are rising, so continuous improvement is required. Kaizen is dedicated to continuous improvement, in small increments, at all levels, forever (!). Everyone has a role, from top management to shop floor employees. Top management must allocate the resources and establish the strategy, systems, procedures and organisational structures necessary for Kaizen to work. Middle managers are responsible for implementing Kaizen. They must monitor performance of the continuous improvement programme, and ensure that employees are educated in the use of the necessary tools. Supervisors are responsible for applying Kaizen. They must maintain the rate of suggestions, coach, and improve communications at the workplace. And shop-floor employees must make suggestions, learn new jobs, use the tools, and generally participate in continuous improvement activities individually and in teams. Imai's book has several examples of how this philosophy works its way down the organisational hierarchy in Japanese companies.

John Shook and later Bill Sandras have made the point that there are two types of kaizen – Flow Kaizen and Point Kaizen. Flow kaizen is about value stream improvement and getting flow going on a cross plant or inter plant basis, or bold changes to streamline a service. Point kaizen are smaller scale opportunities often identified as constraints or low hanging fruit and coming out of mapping activities. Senior management should be more concerned with Flow Kaizen and middle management with point kaizen – however both types should be the concern of all levels.

The Kaizen Flag concept is that there are three activities: innovation (breakthrough), kaizen (ongoing improvement) and following standards. Each level of management needs to do all three but in different quantities. Operators need both to do kaizen and to follow standards. Imai believes that it is the central band of kaizen that makes the difference - but also the extent to which standards are followed. Imai believes that without active attention, the gains made will simply deteriorate (like the engineers' concept of entropy). But Imai goes further. Unlike Juran who emphasises "holding the gains", Kaizen involves building on the gains by continuing experimentation and innovation.

The author believes there is another dimension: "passive" and "enforced" kaizen. Some organisations think they are doing kaizen, but their brand of kaizen is "passive" or left to chance. Improvements are left to the initiative of operators or industrial engineers or managers. If they make improvements - good. If they don't - "oh well, sometime". Passive incremental may also be termed "reactive". A reaction takes place in response to a crisis. By contrast, enforced improvement is proactive. "Crises" are actually engineered and the pressure kept on. For example, Intel brings out a new chip at regular, paced intervals and does not wait passively for technological breakthrough. 3M dictates that 30% of revenues will come from new products every year. Toyota has various "tricks" such as line stop and Andon, kanban withdrawal and waste checklists. This forces the pace.

According to Imai there are several guiding principles. These include:
* Questioning the rules (standards are necessary but work rules are there to be broken and must be broken with time)
* Developing resourcefulness (it is a management priority to develop the resourcefulness and participation of everyone)
* Try to get to the Root Cause (try not to solve problems superficially)
* Eliminate the whole task (question whether a task is necessary; in this respect Kaizen is similar to BPR),
* Reduce or change activities (be aware of opportunities to combine tasks).

The Tools of Kaizen: Kaizen incorporates several tools but the most well known are the Deming Cycle, "5 S", the "5 M Checklist", and the 5 Whys. Also central to Kaizen is the recognition and elimination of waste or Muda (see the section on the Wastes). 5 S and the 5 Whys are described in a separate sections. Visual management is a feature; making operations and quality visible through charts, displayed schedules, kanban, painted designated inventory and tool locations, and the like.

Standards are important in kaizen, to prevent slipping back to old ways. The Kaizen Institute believes there should be periods of consolidation to allow new ways to bed-in, rather than rushing ahead. This idea is absolutely compatible with Deming's "Standardise, Plan, Do, Check" sequence, or Juran's "holding the gains". Standards and Learning are inter-linked. The Joy Manufacturing Company, for instance, communicates value engineering improvements to sites around the world. At Toyota, engineers on new product development make extensive use of checklists. When an engineer learns something new, that knowledge is added to a checklist used for all future vehicles.

Recently, Imai has extended and elaborated on Kaizen in Gemba Kaizen. Gemba means going to the place of action and collecting the facts, rather than sitting in a remote office and collecting opinions.

Kate Mackle former head of the British Kaizen Institute promotes Kaizen through a bottom-up learning process, which eventually permeates the whole organisation. For this a good champion is needed, and Mackle has developed a methodology for identifying suitable people.

Yuso Yasuda has described the Toyota suggestion scheme or "Kaizen system". The scheme is co-ordinated by a "creative idea suggestion committee" whose chairmanship has included Toyota chairmen (Toyoda and Saito) as well as Taiichi Ohno. Rewards for suggestions are given at Toyota based on a points system. Points are scored for tangible and intangible benefits, and for adaptability, creativity, originality, and effort. The rewards are invariably small amounts, and are not based on a percentage of savings. However operators value the token reward and the presentation ceremony itself. Note the contrast with typical Western Suggestion Schemes. Toyota recognises that all suggestions or kaizen ideas may not be beneficial. The Pareto law certainly applies. There will be many ideas that are not really worthwhile, but at the other end of the distribution there will be few hugely beneficial ideas which make the whole scheme very worthwhile. One is reminded of the classic statement about advertising, "I waste half of the money I spend but the problem is I don't which half".

Further reading
Maasaki Imai, *Kaizen: The Key to Japan's Competitive Success*, McGraw Hill, New York, 1986
Maasaki Imai, *Gemba Kaizen*, McGraw Hill, New York, 1997
Yuasa Yasuda, *40 Years, 20 Million Ideas*, Productivity Press, Cambridge MA, 1991

Market Surveys and Customer Observation

All organisations require information about customer needs, expectations, and satisfaction, so market research and surveys are vital. There are several types of market or customer survey but the real issue is to select the right mix and to make sure that information collected is used effectively. For instance, Hewlett Packard uses three linked approaches: A Customer Satisfaction Survey, a Customer Feedback System, and Customer Visits which are carefully integrated for comprehensiveness and efficiency.

But first, consideration needs to be given to which customers should be surveyed. This is not obvious, and depends on the questions you want answered. Candidates are current customers (by spending category, location, need ?), past customers, potential customers, competitor's customers, or customer's customer. Here we consider the major types of survey:

Focus Groups: A small group of customers or potential customers gathered to discuss open-ended questions. Powerful, and can lead down unexpected roads. Requires a skilled facilitator, and may not be representative of customer base, unless particular care is taken. Group members may stimulate one other, to produce further ideas.

Questionnaires: Answers to specific questions are sought. Inexpensive. Low response rate common, requires skilled questionnaire and sample design to be effective and representative. Temptingly easy, but to be meaningful should be first tested on a representative group, validated and statistically justified. Deming and Juran both emphasised that quality is in the eyes of the customer. Therefore a good satisfaction questionnaire should be a two stage process : the first a pilot to determine what it is that are important to customers, and the second to survey opinion. (See also the section on The Performance Importance Matrix).

Interviews: One-on-one talk seeking insights as to why a customer has or has not purchased, or has "defected"; best done close after the event (a new customer, or with a customer where new business has failed to be gained or has been lost). Requires active follow up, skill with defecting customers, and assurance of confidentiality.

Mystery Shopping: A false or posed customer goes through the whole process with your company and with competitors. Not confined to shopping but can be used in any service. Valuable first hand documentation, but possibility of being accused of spying or mistrust.

Customer visits: To check on-site (for example, at a customer's home) on satisfaction levels, and on where and how a product is being used. Questioning users on-site may be very insightful, and may lead to unexpected opportunity. Requires customer goodwill, but is often appreciated by customers.

Debriefing of employees: Surveys show that perhaps three times as many complaints are registered with frontline staff as are received in writing. In many organisations, the views of customers picked up by front-line staff are simply lost. Debriefing must be done in a relaxed, supportive, no-blame atmosphere. Employees may also have good ideas as to new products or services.

Telephone surveys: See questionnaires. May get higher response than mail, but run a risk of greater annoyance.

Freephone (Toll free / Hot line): Making complaining easier. Effective because some problems can be solved immediately, or you are speaking to customers at the time they are actually experiencing problems. This is not the case with questionnaires, for example, and customers are prone to forget detail.

Customer Tours: Customers invited to visit the factory, service facility, bridge of ship or aeroplane. Can create goodwill with high-ticket items and can use the opportunity to discuss reasons for purchase, needs and expectations with captive customers. Confidence and loyalty building.

The Internet: A new source of customer satisfaction data is the internet. These sites have the advantage of assembling frank, uncensored, "from the hip" remarks and experiences. Some include photographs of products that have gone wrong - a well known 4WD vehicle is a case in point. Discussions and evaluations of consumer products and services appear in activity and hobby oriented web pages, and useful information can be obtained from newsgroups. Moreover, newsgroups can be continually monitored, automatically. You will need a search engine such as Google.

Observation: Observation has emerged as a most powerful way of creating innovative products and services, and is therefore particularly relevant for Kano "Performance" and "Delighter" factors. (See the section on the Kano model). Observation can also be combined with some of the previous survey methods, for instance during focus groups, mystery shopping, or customer tours. The method involves close observation, with or without video. Variations are a hidden camera, one-way mirrors, and sound recording. Observation can reveal hidden frustrations and anxieties and difficulties with products and services which customers are reluctant to reveal.

Imprint Analysis: This is a new way of conducting market research which aims at seeking out underlying emotions - the concept being that it is emotion that drives actions and emerging needs. Imprint analysis apparently uses "decoding workshops" involving discussion, word association and relaxation. The true meaning of words to customers and the emotions that result are explored. See Afors and Michaels.

Further reading:
Terry G Vavra, *Improving Your Measurement of Customer Satisfaction*, ASQ Quality Press, Milwaukee, WI, 1997
Byron J Finch, "A New Way to Listen to the Customer", *Quality Progress*, May 1997, pp 73-76
Christina Åfors and Marilyn Zuckerman Michaels, "A Quick Accurate Way to Determine Customer Needs", *Quality Progress*, July 2001, pp 82-87

The Nominal Group Technique (NGT)

The nominal group technique (NGT) is a particular form of team brainstorming and creative problem identification. It is worth specific mention since it is now widely used in place of "classic" brainstorming. NGT is a well researched procedure that draws on both individual and group strengths, using each as appropriate, and which prevents domination by particular individuals. It is a technique that supplements most of the other techniques discussed, and can be used for issue identification, idea generation, and problem solving. NGT has been widely used in quality and productivity improvement and in organizational strategy formulation.

A team is the basic requirement; preferably a multi-level, multi-discipline team. Different disciplines bring different perspectives, and different levels cross the communication boundaries that exist in every organization. A team of between 8 and 12 is considered ideal and there is also a facilitator and perhaps an assistant. The facilitator usually explains to the team how NGT works before the actual process begins.

NGT begins with the facilitator reading out a **statement of the problem** to be tackled by the team. The statement must be carefully prepared and written out, not merely presented "off the cuff". After hearing the statement there are likely to be questions seeking clarification. The facilitator should not now try to revise the problem statement but should encourage the participants to restate the problem in their own words. The facilitator may even nominate two or three members to restate the problem. This is a deliberate stage which forces the team to think through the problem statement in their own words. The facilitator must prevent any team member from dominating, and must not allow the problem to be "hijacked". The original problem statement written out by the facilitator is not altered, it is merely a process of restating in the team's own terms. The facilitator allows discussion to continue until problem formulation, as expressed by the team, seems satisfactory.

The next stage is called **silent generation.** About 15

minutes is allowed for this, during which time silence is required. Each team member is asked to write out his or her responses, alternatives, or suggestions to the problem statement. The team should remain in one room for this purpose since the "atmosphere" of work encourages mental concentration. Team members who may finish early are still required to remain in the room without talking. The silent generation period is used because study has shown that this is the most effective initial way to generate a variety of viewpoints and ideas. The facilitator will discourage talking but may cut short the period if all seem to have completed the task. The facilitator would bring the period to an end, but emphasize that creativity has not stopped and that new ideas can be added to the team member's lists at any time.

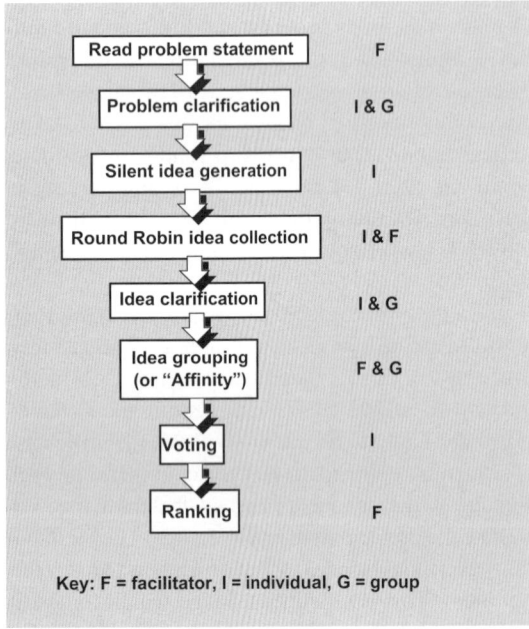

Key: F = facilitator, I = individual, G = group

Now the **"round robin"** stage begins. Each team member is asked in turn to put forward an idea or suggestion. These will usually be taken from team member's lists but not necessarily so. Often, additional ideas will be stimulated by the ideas of others. When each idea is put forward, the facilitator may seek clarification from the team member, but should not change or develop the idea. Other team members are not allowed to participate in these discussions but must wait their turn. No criticism is allowed by team members or the facilitator. As each idea is put forward or clarified is entered onto a chart by the facilitator or an assistant. Only one idea is put forward by each team member before passing onto the next member. Round robin continues until ideas begin to run out and team members say "pass". When there are no more ideas the stage ends.

With all ideas entered onto charts and displayed around the room, the next stage begins. This is called **clarification.** The stage encourages the power of group creativity. The facilitator goes through each suggestion in turn. Once again criticism is not allowed, and each idea is further explained as necessary. Team members may suggest modifications or additions. The team should also group ideas that they consider to be similar (See the section on the Affinity Diagram.) This may result in some deletions and rephrasing. It is important that this stage does not get bogged down in detail, so the facilitator must cut short any rambling discussion. Note: although not part of the original NGT theory, this is the stage at which various creative thinking concepts such as the de Bono "po" word or Roger van Oesch's "Creative Whack Pack" can be used.

The next stage is **selection and ranking**. Blank cards are now issued to all team members and, once again individually and in silence, each member is asked to select the top (say) six ideas. Each member writes the idea on a card together with the ranking at the top of the card. Use 6 for the best idea, and 1 for the lowest chosen idea. Often, team members are asked to alternate as follows. First the top idea of the chosen six is selected and a 6 entered on the card. Then the lowest ranking idea of the six is selected and a 1 written on its card. Then the second best idea is selected and a 5 written on its card, and so on.

The final stage involves the **final ranking.** This is done by the facilitator who gathers the cards and writes the results on a new chart. Next to each idea, transferred from the cards, is written the rankings as given by all the team members. The rankings are anonymous. Each idea will have a string of numbers being the rankings of the team members. There may be several zeros where a team member did not rank an idea in the top six. Now the scores are added up to five the final ranking. In the case of a tie, the idea having the highest number of team member rankings wins.

The result is a ranked set of ideas which, even though there may not be complete team consensus, at least come close to this ideal and which have been generated without dominance by any team member.

Precontrol

Bhote believes that SPC is a technique that should be used with caution. (See the section on SPC). He recommends Precontrol as being faster, easier and in many circustances more valid. Precontrol is still, however, controversial. There is no doubt that its popularity is becoming established in small batch Lean systems.

The procedure is as follows :

1. Divide the tolerance (or specification) band (i.e. the area between the upper and lower tolerance limits) into 4 equal bands. The middle two bands are the green zone (and should be coloured green on a chart). The two outer areas are called the yellow zone. Beyond the tolerance limits is the red band.
2. Following Changeover (to check capability) : Measure 5 consecutive units.
   If all five are in the green zone, the process is in control. Production can start.
   If even one is in the red zone, the process is not in control. Production must not start. Reset the process.
   If one is in the yellow zone, a 'special cause' may be present. Take another sample of 5. Better still, investigate.
   If two consecutive readings fall in the yellow zone, adjust the process and restart the measurement process.
3. During production : Take samples of two consecutive units.
   If even one unit falls in the red zone, stop production and investigate. Return to Step 2.
   If both units fall in the yellow zones, stop production and investigate. Return to Step 2.
   If one unit falls in the yellow zone and one in the green, continue.
   If both units fall in the green, continue.
4. Sample 6 pairs between setups. (e.g. for an hour long batch, sample on average every 10 minutes)

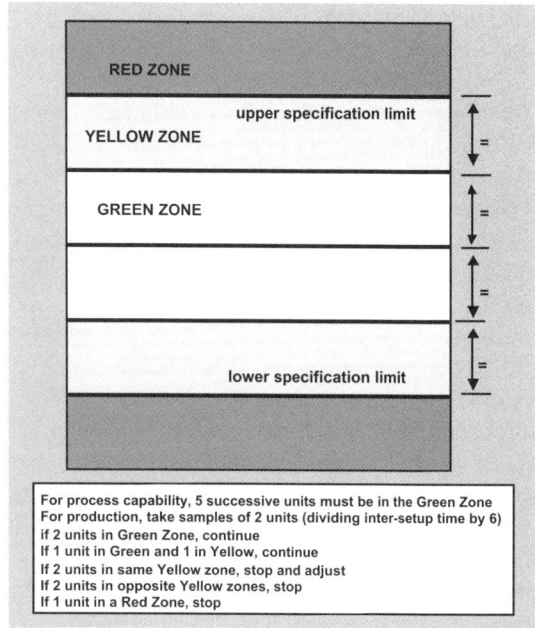

For process capability, 5 successive units must be in the Green Zone
For production, take samples of 2 units (dividing inter-setup time by 6)
If 2 units in Green Zone, continue
If 1 unit in Green and 1 in Yellow, continue
If 2 units in same Yellow zone, stop and adjust
If 2 units in opposite Yellow zones, stop
If 1 unit in a Red Zone, stop

The method is obviously very simple. Precontrol charts can be printed ahead of time and no statistical training is necessary. Implementation is immediate. However, critics have pointed out that Precontrol is based on tolerance limits, not on process variation as is the case with SPC. As such the method relies on these tolerances being carefully set during design. Some statisticians have pointed out that a sample size of 2 may simply be inadequate. Nevertheless, the technique is statistically based and is likely to be reliable under many circumstances.

Further reading:
Dorian and Peter Shainin, "Precontrol versus X and R Charting", *Quality Engineering*, Vol 1 No 4, 1989.
Keki R Bhote and Adi Bhote, *World Class Quality*, AMACOM, 2000, Chapter 21.

The Process Model and PETS

The elements of the process model are Supplier, Input, Process, Output, and Customer. This is the basic building block for any process, and as such should be held in the mind of anyone at any level attempting a process improvement. It helps maintain the "helicopter" vision of a process. Supply chains are made up of strings of these interlocking elements and are only as good as the weakest link. Draw it out as a block diagram. Start at the customer end:

Customer – are you clear who the ultimate customer is; do you understand their true requirements and demands; how loyal; how satisfied; how measured?

Output – what is produced, is it appropriate to the customer; does it meet requirements for cost, quality, quantity, time? For example, an output may be a product but may also be a satisfied customer. Note the invisible outputs such as satisfaction or hostility from "trapped" customers. What measures are appropriate – cost, quality, delivery, safety?

Process – the means by which input is transformed into output. Will usually contain sub processes of both physical and information flows. What is the yield, the Overall Equipment Effectiveness (OEE)? Processes can be looked at using the PETS mnemonic: Are the Procedures clear? Is the Equipment capable of doing the job? Has adequate Training been done? And are the Standards known and clear?

Inputs – the "men, methods, machines, materials, measures, mother nature, and information" Are these to spec? Note there may be invisible inputs such as staff who keep the place running by goodwill.

Suppliers – who are they; have you communicated the requirements clearly; is partnership appropriate? Is supply reliable? How is it measured – in terms of quality, quantity, and timing?

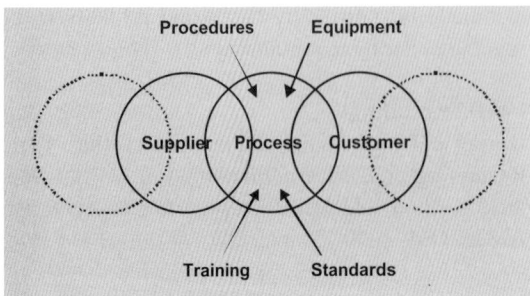

Quality Function Deployment (QFD)

Quality Function Deployment is a "meta" technique that has gown hugely in importance over the last decade and is now used in both product and service design. It is a meta technique because many other techniques described in this book can or should be used in undertaking QFD design or analysis. These other techniques include several of the "new tools", benchmarking, market surveys, the Kano model, the performance - importance matrix, and FMEA.

Customer needs are identified and systematically compared with the technical or operating characteristics of the product or service. The process brings out the relative importance of customer needs which, when set against the characteristics of the product leads to the identification of the most important or sensitive characteristics. These are the characteristics which need development or attention. Although the word "product" is used in the descriptions which follow, QFD is equally applicable in services. Technical characteristics then become the service characteristics.

Perhaps a chief advantage of QFD is that it is carried out by a multi-disciplinary team all concerned with the particular product. QFD acts as a forum for marketing, design, engineering, manufacturing, distribution and others to work together using a concurrent or simultaneous engineering approach. QFD is then the vehicle for these specialists to attack a problem together rather than by "throwing the design over the wall" to the next stage. QFD is therefore not only concerned with quality but with the simultaneous objectives of reducing overall development time, meeting customer requirements, reducing cost, and producing a product or service which fits together and works well the first time. The mechanics of QFD are not cast in stone, and can easily be adapted to local innovation.

The first QFD matrix is also referred to as the "house of quality". This is because of the way the matrices in QFD fit together to form a house-shaped diagram. A full QFD exercise may deploy several matrix diagrams, forming a sequence which gradually translates customer requirements into specific manufacturing steps and detailed manufacturing process requirements. For instance, a complete new car could be considered at the top level but subsequent exercises may be concerned with the engine, body shell, doors, instrumentation, brakes, and so on. Thereafter the detail would be deployed into manufacturing and production. But the most basic QFD exercise would use only one matrix diagram which seeks to take customer requirements and to translate them into specific technical requirements.

The "House of Quality" Diagram

In the sections opposite the essential composition of the basic house of quality diagram is explained. Refer to the figure.

Customer requirements

The usual starting point for QFD is the identification of customer needs and benefits. This is also referred to as "the voice of the customer" or "the whats". Customers may be present or future, internal or external, primary or secondary. All the conventional tools of marketing research are relevant, as well as techniques such as complaint analysis and focus groups. Customers may include owners, users, and maintainers, all of whom have separate requirements. Refer to the section on market research. After collection comes the problem of how to assemble the information before entering it into the rows. In this the "new tools" of affinity and tree diagrams have been found to be especially useful. This results in a hierarchy; on the primary level are the broad customer requirements, with the secondary requirements adding the detail.

Marketing would have responsibility for assembling much of the customer information, but the team puts it together. Marketing may begin by circulating the results of surveys and by a briefing. It is important to preserve the "voice of the customer", but the team may group like requirements using the affinity diagram. The team must not try to "second guess" or to assume that they know best what is needed by customers.

Rankings or relative importance of customer requirements

When the customer requirements are assembled onto the matrix on the left of the house diagram, weightings are added on the right to indicate the importance of each requirement. Weightings are established by market research or focus groups or, failing these, the team may determine rankings by a technique such as "pairwise comparison". (In pairwise comparison, each requirement is compared with each other. The most important of the two requirements gains a point, and all scores are added up to determine final rankings.) The Kano model (see separate section) is very often used with QFD as an aid in determining appropriate weightings.

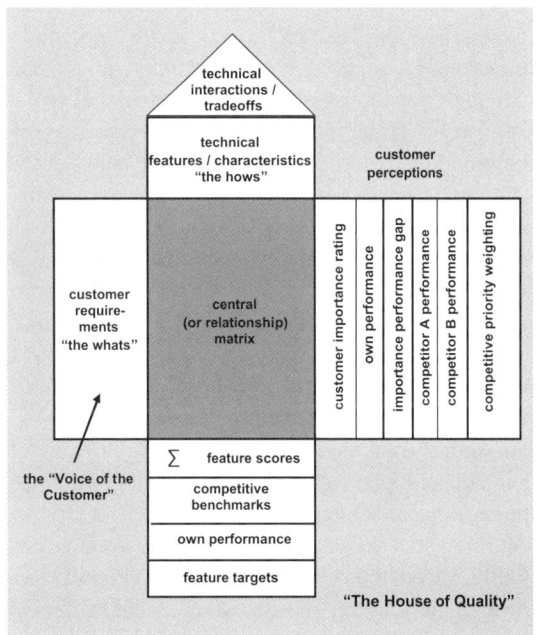

"The House of Quality"

Technical characteristics and associated rankings

Customer requirements and weightings are displayed in rows. The technical characteristics (or "hows" or "technical responses") form the columns. These characteristics are the features that the organisation provides in the design to respond to the customer requirements (For a kettle this may include power used, strength of the materials, insulation, sealing, materials used, and noise.) Once again these could be assembled into groups to form a hierarchy, using the Tree Diagram. Here the team will rely on its own internal expertise. There are at least two ways to develop technical characteristics. On way is go via measures that respond to customer needs. For instance a customer need for the kettle may be "quick boil". The measure is "minutes to boil" and the technical response is the power of the heating element. Another is to go directly to functions, based on the teams experience or on current technology.

The Planning Matrix

To the right of the central matrix is found the planning matrix. This is a series of columns which evaluate the importance, satisfaction, and goal for each customer need. (See the figure). The first column shows importance to the customer of each need. Here a group of customers may be asked to evaluate the importance of each need on a 1 to 5 scale (1=not important, 5=vital, of highest importance). In the next column the current performance of each product or service need, is rated by the group of customers. The difference between the columns is the gap - a negative number indicates possible overprovision, a positive number indicates a shortfall. The reader will recognise that here the QFD process is duplicating the importance-performance matrix (see separate section), or the SERVQUAL gaps. The next few columns give the competitors current performance on each customer need. The aim of this part of the exercise is to clearly identify the "SWOT" (strengths, weaknesses, opportunities, threats) of competitor products as against your own. For example, the kettle manufacturer may be well known for product sturdiness, but be weak on economy. If economy is highly ranked, this will point out an opportunity and, through the central matrix, show what technical characteristics can be used to make up this deficiency. The gap (if any) between own and competitors performance can then be determined. Since the QFD team now has detail on the gap for each need and of the importance of each need, they can then decide the desired goal for each customer need - normally expressed in the same units as the performance column. Deciding the goal for each need is an important task for the QFD team. These goals are the weights to be used in the relationship matrix. (Note : in some versions of QFD there are additional columns).

The Central (or Relationship) Matrix

The central matrix lies at the heart of the house of quality diagram. This is where customer needs are matched against each technical characteristic. The nature of the relationship is noted in the matrix by an appropriate symbol. The team can devise their own symbols; for instance, numbers may indicate the relative strength of the relationship or simply ticks may suffice. The strength of the relationship or impact is recorded in the matrix. These relationships may be nil, possibly linked, moderately linked or strongly linked. Corresponding weights (typically 0, 1, 3, 9) are assigned . Thereafter the scores for each technical characteristic are determined as in the "new tool" of Matrix Analysis (refer to the section in this book which details how a total score is determined for each characteristic). This matching exercise is carried out by the team based on their experience and judgement. The idea is to clearly identify all means by which the "whats" can be achieved by the "hows". It will also check if all "whats" can in fact be achieved (insufficient technical characteristics?), and if some technical characteristics are not apparently doing anything (redundancy?). A blank row indicates a customer requirement not met. A blank column indicates a redundant technical feature. In practice, matrix evaluation can be a very large task (a moderate size QFD matrix of 30 x 30 has 900 cells to be evaluated). The team may split the task between them.

Technical Matrix

Immediately below the relationship matrix appears one or more rows for rankings such as cost or technical difficulty or development time. The choice of these is dependent on the product. These will enable the team to judge the efficacy of various technical solutions. The prime row uses the customer weightings and central matrix to derive the relative technical characteristic rankings. A full example is given under Matrix Analysis in the New Tools section of this booklet.

Next below the relationship matrix comes one or more rows for competitive evaluation. Here, where possible, "hard" data is used to compare the actual physical or engineering characteristics of your product against those of competitors. In the kettle example these would include watts of electricity, mass, and thermal conductivity of the kettle walls. This is where benchmarking is done. By now the QFD team will know the critical technical characteristics, and these should be benchmarked against competitors (See the section on Benchmarking - especially competitive benchmarking). So to the right of the relationship matrix one can judge relative customer perceptions and below the relative technical performance.

The bottom row of the house, which is also the "bottom line" of the QFD process, are the target technical characteristics. These are expressed in physical terms and are decided upon after team discussion of the complete house contents, as described below. The target characteristics are, for some, the final output of the exercise, but many would agree that it is the whole process of information assembly, ranking, and team discussion that goes into QFD which is the real benefit, so that the real output is improved inter-functional understanding.

The roof of the house

The roof of the house is the technical interaction matrix. The diagonal format allows each technical characteristic to be viewed against each other one. This simply reflects any technical trade-offs that may exist. For example with the kettle two technical characteristics may be insulation ability and water capacity. These have a negative relationship; increasing the insulation decreases the capacity. These interactions are made explicit, using the technical knowledge and experience of the team. Some cells may highlight challenging technical issues - for instance thin insulation in a kettle, which may be the subject of R&D work leading to competitive advantage. The roof is therefore useful to highlight areas in which R&D work could best be focused.

Using the house as a decision tool

The central matrix shows what the required technical characteristics are that will need design attention. The costs of these can be seen with reference to the base rows. This may have the effect of shifting priorities if costs are important. Then the technical trade-offs are examined. Often there will be more than one technical way to impact a particular customer requirement, and this is clear from rows in the matrix. And it may also be that one technical alternative has a negative influence on another customer requirement. This is found out by using the roof matrix. Eventually, through a process of team discussion, a team consensus will emerge. This may take some time, but experience shows that time and cost is repaid many times over as the actual design, engineering and manufacturing steps proceed.

The bottom line is now the target values of technical characteristics. This set can now go into the next house diagram. This time the target technical characteristics become the "customer requirements" or "whats", and the new vertical columns (or "hows") are, perhaps, the technologies, the assemblies, the materials, or the layouts. And so the process "deploys" until the team feels that sufficient detail has been considered to cover all coordination considerations in the process of bringing the product to market.

Note: QFD may be used in several stages in order to "deploy" customer requirements all the way to the final manufacturing or procedural stages. Here the outcome of one QFD matrix (e.g. the technical specifications), becomes the input into the next matrix which may aim to look at process specifications to make the product.

Assembling the team

A QFD team should have up to a dozen members with representation from all sections concerned with the development and launch of the product. Team composition may vary depending on whether new products or the improvement of existing products is under consideration. The important thing is that there is representation from all relevant sections and disciplines. There may well be a case for bringing in outsiders to stimulate the creative process and to ask the "silly" questions. Team members must have the support of their section heads. These section heads may feel it necessary to form a steering group. QFD teams are not usually full time, but must be given sufficient time priority to avoid time clashes. The team leader may be full time for an important QFD. The essential characteristics are team leadership skills rather than a particular branch of knowledge.

Relationship with other techniques

As mentioned. QFD is a "meta" technique in that several other techniques can be fitted in with it. For example, value management may be used to explore some of the technical alternatives, costs and trade-offs in greater detail. Taguchi analysis is commonly used with QFD because it is ideally suited to examining the most sensitive engineering characteristics so as to produce a robust design. Failure mode and effect analysis (FMEA) can be used to examine consequences of failure, and so to throw more light on the technical interactions matrix. And mention has already been made of the use of various "New Tools". In the way the QFD team carries out its work, weights alternatives, generates alternatives, groups characteristics, and so on, there are many possibilities. QFD only provides the broad concept. There is much opportunity for adaptation and innovation.

Further reading:
Ronald G. Day, *Quality Function Deployment*, ASQ Quality Press, Milwaukee, WI, 1994
Lou Cohen, *Quality Function Deployment : How to make QFD work for you*, Addison Wesley, Reading MA, 1995
Jack B ReVelle et al., *The QFD Handbook*, ASQ Quality Press, 1998

Single Point Lessons

A single point lesson is a useful way to tackle short, specific issues of importance or persistent quality issues. It is a different form of education. A single point lesson is simply a chart, placed at the point of use (at "Gemba") to illustrate one single new procedure. Examples may be a start up procedure for a machine, a regular check that must be carried out, the right way to dispatch a parcel, to manage kanban, or do any other standard operation. Usually a picture is incorporated as well as the stages of learning the procedure. Instead of sitting in a classroom learning a whole host of new concepts, most of which are soon forgotten, a single point lesson aims to teach new things of short duration at the point of use, by repetition.

Learning and short duration are significant points. The procedure should take a maximum of 15 minutes, frequently far less. The chart acts as a reminder and reinforcer. After basic instruction is given the chart is placed at the point of use for staff or operators to refer to. An instructor or manager would occasionally come around and test for compliance. When staff has demonstrated repeated competence the chart is removed. Stages are marked on the chart, frequently using a colour-in pie to indicate beginner, early learner, competent, master.

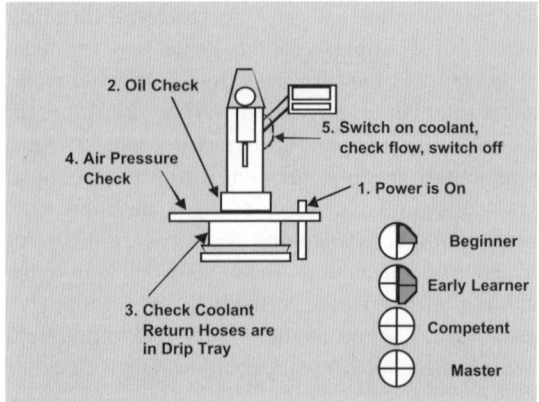

A single point lesson is not a standard operating procedure which should remain at the point of use permanently and which does not aim at learning.

Supplier Partnerships

The concept of supplier partners developed strongly in the 1990's as a result of the movement towards lean manufacturing. Lean emphasises reduction in waste, shortening of lead times, improvement in quality, continuous improvement, and simplicity. These are the goals of supplier partnership, also. Today supplier partnerships are found both in service and manufacturing.

The philosophy is that, through cooperation rather than confrontation, both parties benefit. It is a longer term view, emphasising total cost rather than product price. Cost includes not only today's price of the part or product, but also its quality (ppm rate), delivery reliability, delivery frequency, the simplicity with which the transaction is processed, and the future potential for price reductions.

But partnership goes further: long term, stable relationships are sought rather than short term, adversarial, quick advantage transactions. The analogy of a marriage is often used. It may have its ups and downs, but commitment remains. In a partnership, contracts will be longer term to give the supplier confidence and the motivation to invest and improve. Both parties recognise that the game whereby low prices are bid and then argued up on contingencies once the contract is awarded, is wasteful and counterproductive. Instead, it may be possible for both parties to cooperate on price reduction, sharing the benefits between them. Such cooperation may be achieved through the temporary secondment of staff.

For partnership to work, there must of necessity be few or single suppliers per part. There is small risk of "being taken for a ride" because there is too much for a supplier to lose, and much to gain. There may however be a risk of disruption in supply. This should be a calculated risk; where the probability is very small the advantages of a single supplier may outweigh the risks. And there are ways around this too : having one supplier exclusively supplying a part to one plant, but another supplier exclusively supplying the same part to another plant. This spreads the risk whilst still achieving single supplier advantages.

Alternatively there is the Japanese practice of cultivating several suppliers simultaneously but then awarding an exclusive contract to one supplier of a part for the life of the product, and selecting another supplier for a similar part going into another end product. The idea is to work with a few good, trusted suppliers who supply a wide range of parts. Partnership has therefore resulted in drastic reductions in many a company's supplier base. An objective is to remove the long tail of the supplier Pareto curve whereby perhaps 10% of parts are supplied by 80% of the suppliers. Often it will be found that a large number of suppliers supply a very small proportion of value. Then, exploration as to how to reduce or combine sourcing begins. Award business to those identified as potential partners, and gradually drop the rest. Supplier days are held, often annually, when company plans and objectives are explained, measures given, prizes for best performance given out, and factory tours held. For true partnership, director level meetings are held periodically, with much more frequent manager and engineer contact.

On quality, a partnership aims at zero receiving inspection and delivery directly to the point of use. Packaging and part orientation may be specifically designed to reduce waste. Delivery would often be subject to kanban call-off : the partner would be given long term forecasts of gross requirements far out, more detailed requirements close in, but the actual sequence and timing of delivery is controlled by kanban. Both sides need to work towards schedule stability and avoiding "demand amplification" and the "Forrester Effect". This requires communication of demand right along the supply chain, and coordinated schedules. The point is, there should be advantages for both sides : unstable schedules ultimately cost the customer in terms of money and risk, and reduce the possibility of productivity gain at the supplier.

Sometimes, the supplier is responsible for maintaining inventory levels at a customer, called VMI (vendor managed inventory) which is increasingly found for consumables. Other times, a manufacturer may write the production schedule of the supplier. As trust builds, self billing or reconciliation becomes possible ("we built 100 cars, so here is our cheque for the 500 tyres we must have used"). An advanced form is "JITII" (a registered mark of the Bose corporation) whereby a few major suppliers have full time representatives in the host plant, with access to company records and schedules, and whose responsibilities include writing purchase orders on their own company. Such reps also participate in design work and R&D, and attend company planning meetings. JITII is now beginning to be found outside of Bose in companies such as Hewlett Packard and Intel. These partnership arrangements stem from the interesting insight of Lance Dixon that it is actually more secure to have a supplier write purchase orders on himself than it is for one of your own staff to do so (because legal action can recover damages from a supplier resulting from negligence, but seldom can be recovered from your own employee!).

Improved communication links via EDI or EPOS further enhance partnership advantages. Delivery cooperation becomes possible either through "milkrounds" (whereby small quantities are collected from several firms in an area every day, rather than from one firm once per week), or, where more work is given to one supplier, mixed loads are sent every day rather than one-product loads once per week. This improves flow and reduces inventories.

Cooperation on design is part of partnership. The manufacturer recognises the supplier's ability to design the parts that it makes, rather than simply specifying. This policy of "open specs" or "black box" specs can lead to faster product development, lower cost, and more up to date part supply. The partnership idea encourages the concept of a company sticking to its core business, whilst putting out non-core business.

Generally, supplier partnership makes sense for "A" and possibly "B" parts; less so for commodity items. Part criticality and risk also influence the partnership decision; you would not risk partnership with a company having poor industrial relations, or weak finances, or poor quality assurance. This means that a team approach is necessary in supplier selection. The Purchasing Officer may coordinate, but throughout the partnership Design would talk to their opposite number in Design, Quality to Quality, Production control to Production control, and so on.

Disadvantages ? Time, commitment, costs of establishment, risk of inappropriate choices of partner, and short term cost reduction opportunities foregone against medium term gains.

Value engineering is a technique that both parties may adopt for mutual advantage. VE/VA is a powerful technique for cost, quality and delivery. In advanced partnerships a "satellite plant" dedicated to a particular customer and located nearby, or "suppliers in residence" where the supplier's operation and or some of its staff are permanently located on the customer's site, may be worth consideration. Volkswagen's Brazilian plants are reported to use supplier's employees on the VW assembly line - is this the future of partnership, or a quest for flexibility?

In Japan, and increasingly in the rest of the world, supplier partnership is now expanding down from relationships with first tier suppliers, to second and even third tier. Supplier associations are being established. These are "clubs" established to share the strengths of members. The thought, in common with TQM, is that quality is only as good as the weakest link in the supply chain or network.

Further reading:
James Womack, Daniel Jones, Daniel Roos, *The Machine that Changed the World*, Rawson Associates, New York, 1990, Chapter 6.
Peter Hines and David Taylor, *Going Lean*, 2000, Available via www. cf.ac.uk/carbs/lerc
Peter Hines, *Creating World Class Suppliers : Unlocking mutual competitive advantage*, Pitman, London, 1994,
Richard Lamming, *Beyond Partnership*, Prentice Hall, Hemel Hempstead, 1993,
Lance Dixon and Anne Millen Porter, *JITII : Revolution in Buying and Selling*, Purchasing Magazine / Cahners, Newton, MA, 1994

Sustainability

Implementing quality improvements is one thing. Sustaining the improvement is quite another. The field of TQM, Kaizen, Business Process Reengineering, and Lean is littered with failure. Here we attempt some guidelines to avoid slipping back.

* Sustainability begins before any change event with preparing the ground. Recognise that there is a threat to people who have been doing a job for perhaps many years. These people are not necessarily reactionary but may well be justifiably cautious. Take time to explain but also to seek their help and involvement
* Sustainability is not about techniques; it is about people
* Change generates antibodies that automatically grow to fight the change. This is like Newton's Third Law – for every action there is an equal and opposite reaction. The antibodies need to be managed or the fever will not take hold. Those in favour of change may be neutralised. So identify the antibodies as early as possible. Inject them. Antibodies that continue to react need to be moved out decisively and quickly

Bateman lists the following "enablers" for sustainability, based on her research
* There should be a formal way of documenting ideas from the shop floor
* Ensure that operators make decisions in a team about the way they work
* Make sure there is time dedicated to (housekeeping) every day
* Ensure there are measures to monitor the improvements made, at an appropriate level
* Managers should stay focused on improvement activities

And for yet higher gains she recommends
* Changes to operating methods should be formally introduced to all (?) members - including those not taking part in the improvement

* The area should have a strategy – for people to appreciate the big picture
* There should be a person co-ordinating improvement activities across the whole site
* Senior managers should be involved in improvement activities
* Senior management should stay focused on improvement activities – by reviewing progress as a whole and not imposing unnecessary initiatives

Choi lists the pitfalls of improvement initiatives, based on his research, as
* Alienation of line leaders (both on involvement and improvement being seen as interfering with performance)
* Seeing improvement as the same as regular problem-solving activity – which confuses those outside and inside
* Identifying improvement teams as special – thereby building resentment
* Seeing improvement as a management programme – bypassing workers
* Seeing improvement as solely a worker thing – lacking communication, interest, and involvement from above
* Intermittent – stop go initiatives – here we go again

Standard and Davis suggest that sustaining a transformation requires
* A formalised organisational structure – like a kaizen office
* A higher degree of job specialisation – begin with deeper skills, and only later on cross training
* An organisation structure with few levels – to aid cross-functional communication and to keep 'close to the action'

Military intelligence officers know that a situation is only dangerous when there is capability and intention. Both are necessary; otherwise there is no danger. The same goes for sustainability – there must be both the capability (time, resources) and the intention (determination, drive, and insistence).

Two theories from change management seem relevant. "Cognitive Dissonance" says that people try to be consistent in attitude and behaviour. Thus if a change is out of kilter with prevailing attitudes it will fail. The "psychological contract" says that there is an unwritten implicit set of expectations (covering, for instance, a sense of dignity and worth) which if breached will lead to disruption and implementation failure.

Finally all who attempt change should spend 40 minutes reading the marvellous little book by Dr Spenser Johnson, *Who Moved My Cheese?*, about the two mice and the small people. Which of them, Sniff, Scurry, Hem, or Haw, are you?

Further reading
Nicola Bateman, *Sustainability*, Lean Enterprise Research Centre, Cardiff Business School, Wales, April 2001
Thomas Choi, "The Successes and Failures of Implementing Continuous Improvement Programs', in Jeff Liker (ed), *Becoming Lean*, Productivity Press, Portland, 1998
Charles Standard and Dale Davis, *Running Today's Factory*, Hanser Gardner, Cincinnati, 1999, Chapter 13
Bernard Burns, *Managing Change*, Third edition, FT/Pitman, Harlow, 2000, Chapter 12
Spenser Johnson, *Who Moved My Cheese?*, Vermillion, London, 1998

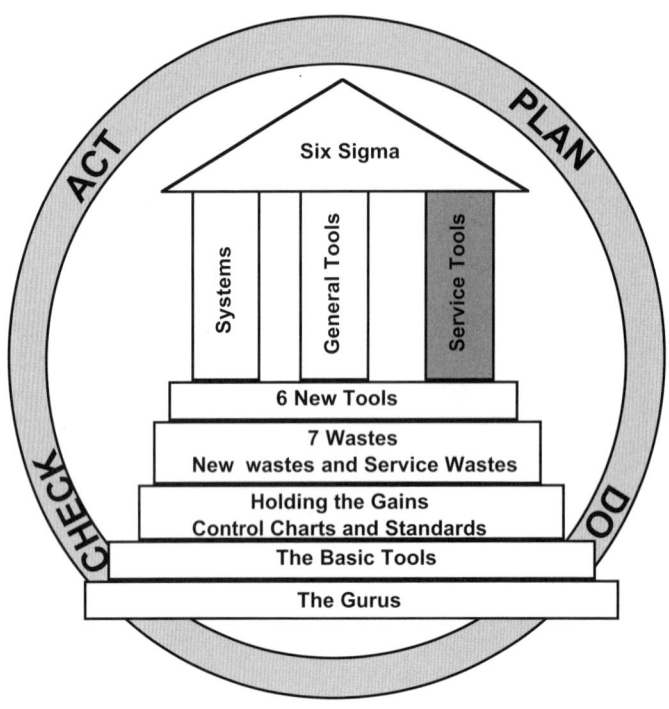

Service Tools

Service Mapping
Cycle of Service and Customer Processing Operation
Moments of Truth
Service Blueprinting

Other Service Tools
Customer Loyalty
Service Gaps, SERVQUAL, and Service Dimensions
Service Profit Chain
Service Recovery and Customer Retention
Zone of Tolerance

Cycle of Service and Customer Processing Operation

Albrecht and Zemke originated the concept of a Cycle of Service, but the idea has been added to by Mahesh and by Vandermerwe. The Customer Processing concept is a variation, developed by Johnston.

A Cycle of Service (C of S) is much like a flowchart but has the important distinction of being written from the perspective of the customer, and is the sequence of events or "Moments of Truth" (MoT) (see section on this topic) experienced by the customer in dealing with the organisation. After all, as Vandermerwe suggests, value is associated with the customer, but providers only accumulate costs. As the name suggests, a C of S is normally shown on a circle. A flowchart shows the progress of a document or product, a cycle of service shows the events experienced by a customer. It is simple but effective.

The best way to draw up a cycle of service is to physically track a customer as he or she moves through a service process. Of course, not all customers will experience the same Moments of Truth, so several customer experiences may have to be combined. Where customer tracking is not possible, a team of front line employees should participate in drawing up the chart. It is best to use the verb plus noun rule in drawing up a C of S chart : for instance, "receive notice", "join queue", and the like.

Then analysis begins. Points of dissatisfaction are identified. The value of the C of S is that, perhaps for the first time, the complete sequence of events as experienced by the customer, is seen. A useful starting point is the "PETS" framework : ask, for each moment of truth, if the Procedure is known, if the Equipment is suitable or capable of doing the job, if Training has been adequate, and if Standards are in place. Some of the MoTs will be more important than others, and will require much more attention. Where necessary, any MoT can be further broken down into a greater level of detail. For instance, the MoT "receive bank balance", can be broken down into "wait for chit", "receive chit from teller", "open chit", "read balance and other information".

Thereafter the Kano model is extremely useful. (See the section on Kano.) Ask, for each MoT, what are the Basics, the Performance factors, and possible Delighters. This is a useful way of undertaking systematic analysis of weaknesses and of opportunities. The section on the Kano model emphasised that the identification of the three Kano factors is not necessarily trivial; good analysis and insight may only be gained by detailed observation.

In addition we can consider how or if each MoT can be failsafed (see the section on Shingo or Pokayoke). Recall the methods of failsafing : by contact (a height barrier in a car park), by fixed value (an airline meal tray with indentations), and by motion step (a customer number at a supermarket "deli" to ensure first come first serve).

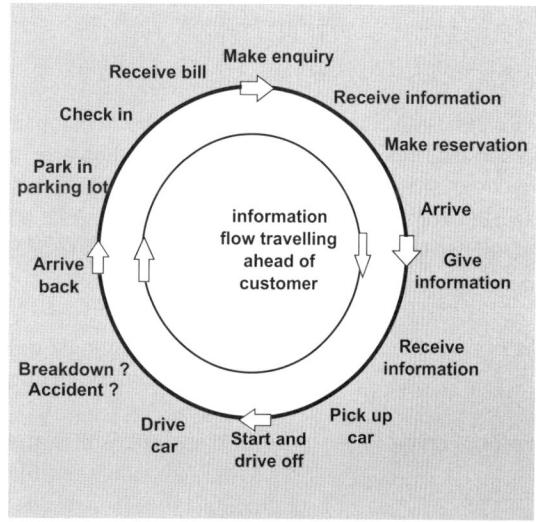

Sandra Vandermerwe's version of C of S is referred to as the Customer Activity Cycle (or CAC). This has the extension of considering "Pre", "During", and "Post" activities. Vandermerwe makes the point that customer's experiences span three stages : deciding what to do, doing it, and keeping it going and updating it. This is therefore a more powerful version because it is not limited to the actual service encounter itself. The tool acts as an agitation and educational device according to Vandermerwe. She refers to discontinuities in the flow of the cycle as "value gaps", a phrase which suggests that closing such gaps may find the framework suggested by Zeithaml et al (see the section on SERVQUAL) useful. As with the breakdown of the C of S into a hierarchy of detail, the CAC has "primary cycles", "dependent cycles" and "sub cycles".

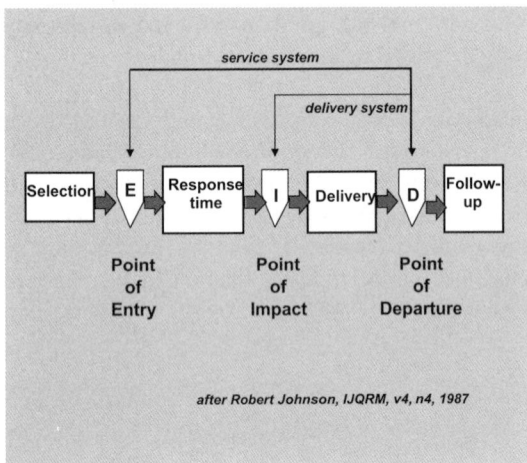

after Robert Johnson, IJQRM, v4, n4, 1987

The Johnston variation (known as the "customer processing operation" or CPO) is not shown as a cycle or a map but rather as a framework or checklist. The elements are useful in clarifying the stages, and could easily be incorporated in the previous C of S approaches. The elements are:

Selection:	when the customer decides between competing services.
Point of entry:	the initial assessment, the visual impact, possible confusion for a new customer.
Response time:	the time taken to respond, waiting, queuing
Point of Impact:	the first point of contact and initial impression
Delivery:	the actual events (MoTs?) of the service itself
Point of Departure:	any special events or opportunities when the customer leaves
Follow up:	obtaining feedback on satisfaction, or soliciting further business.

Further reading

G Lynn Shostack, "Designing Services that Deliver", *Harvard Business Review*, Vol 64, January / February 1984, pages 133-139

Vandermerwe, Sandra *The Eleventh Commandment*, Wiley, Chichester 1996, Chap 23

Mahesh, V.S. and Stanworth, James "Service Concept Delivery through System Design : The Case of Anglian Water Services", *Service Management : New perspectives, New initiatives*, C. Armistead and R. Teare (eds), Cassell, London, 1995

Robert Johnston, "A framework for delivering quality strategy in the customer processing operation", *Int Jnl of Quality and Reliability Mgmt*, 4, 4, 1987, pp 37-46

Moments of Truth (MoT)

Moments of truth (MoT) is a concept rather than a technique, apparently first articulated by Jan Carlzon, the head of the Scandinavian airline SAS. It is a powerful concept for quality management, and so deserves a place in any gallery of quality concepts. The concept was made even more popular by Albrect and Zemke in their book "Service America!"

A moment of truth is that moment in time when a customer comes into contact with the products, systems, people, or procedures of an organization and as a result is lead to make a judgement about the quality of that organization's products or services.

It is clear that scores, even hundreds, of MoTs are possible for a single customer in interaction with a company. Each one is a potential point of dissatisfaction where, as a result, the customer may be lost, or conversely where the customer can experience "delight" and become a loyal user. Some MoTs are critical, others less so, and here it is useful to bring in the Kano model concepts (see separate section). Moreover, the customer builds an impression of the organisation through the cumulative effect of MoT experiences. In many services (eg hotels, holidays, travel, parcel delivery, banking, consultancy) the customer has little or no tangible product that remains after the operation is complete. All that the customer is left with is a memory - of hundreds of moments of truth. That is why the proactive analysis of MoTs should be an important concern of management, particularly if they believe that it costs five times as much to regain a lost customer as it does to acquire a new one.

This leads to MoT analysis where the points of potential dissatisfaction can be proactively identified. MoT analysis begins with the assembly of process-type diagrams (these are referred to as "cycles of service"; see separate section). Every minute step taken by a customer in his or her dealings with company products, services or people is recorded. This begins when the customer first makes contact (perhaps by telephone, mail, or in person) to the last time the product or service is experienced. There would be a different chart for each type of customer service. Whether called a process chart or a cycle of service, the point is that the steps follow the experiences of the customer, irrespective of organizational boundaries or departments.

The problem from a quality management viewpoint is that most MoTs take place away from the eyes of management, but in interaction with the "front line" staff. All MoTs occur with either the visible product or with the front line - with the latter by far the predominant case in the case of service industry. That is why it is desirable to work through all possible MoTs in advance. It is said that, even if a product or service fails, if the backup service is good the customer will not be resentful and may even be grateful. One may argue that it is not possible to identify all MoTs, but at least if a systematic effort has been made the number and severity of unexpected failures will be minimized. In this respect MoT analysis has much in common with failure mode and effect analysis (FMEA).

Further reading:
Jan Carlzon, *Moments of Truth*, Harper and Row, 1987
Christian Grönroos, *Service Management and Marketing : Managing the Moments of Truth in Service Competition*, Lexinngton Books, MA, 1990

Service Blueprinting

Service blueprinting is the procedure of making a flowchart or map of a service process. This is one the longest established service mapping tools and was originally proposed by Shostack. The technique has much in common with industrial engineering flowcharts, except that customer links are specifically included. The aim is to identify points at which the service may fail to satisfy customers and to identify points where value may be added for customers. A service blueprint shows time horizontally, and the hierarchy of support vertically. In drawing up a blueprint, four areas are included :

* "customer actions" are the activities or interactions undertaken by the customer. These activities come into contact with two types of employee actions:
* "on stage" employee actions are visible to the customer and are separated in a service blueprint by a "line of interaction", drawn horizontally. Any vertical line crossing this line of interaction represents a direct contact or encounter between customer and front line employee.
* "backstage" employee actions are not visible to customers but are nevertheless in direct contact with customers (say by post or phone). These are separated from on stage activities by a "line of visibility", thus making clear what customers can see and possibly be influenced by.
* "support processes" are all those activities that support the front-line staff, whether visible or not. These are separated from backstage activities by a "line of internal interaction". Vertical lines crossing the line of internal interaction represent internal encounters.

A service blueprint can be read horizontally to focus on customer support activities and to answer questions such as how efficient, and how many points of contact are involved. Alternatively, a blueprint can be used to gain an overview or to understand the depth and nature of the support infrastructure, in which case it is read vertically. An immediate impression of the complexity of the service process is given by a blueprint, as are the steps that a customer faces in dealing with an organisation. An illustration is shown in the figure.

**SERVICE BLUEPRINTING
Student Registration Example**

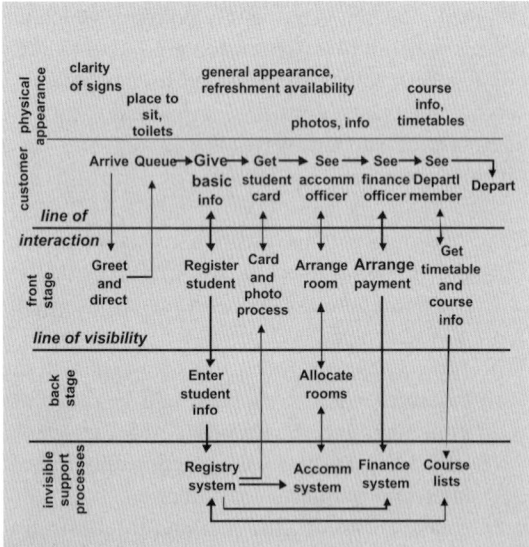

The power of service blueprints can be added to by including "pre", and "post" activities, pokayoke, and the Kano model. (See the section on Cycle of Service and Customer processing.) A service blueprint can be a particularly good device for training or standardisation purposes, where photos can be added. Service can be standardised by maintaining the up-to-date position on a computer service blueprint, possibly supported by digital photo or even video. Think of two accompanying charts. The first is the "Spaghetti Diagram" showing the physical movements of customers and servers (shown in different colours). The second chart lists, for each activity in the customer line, the Kano factors (Basics, Performance, Delighters), and possible failsafing or pokayoke. See separate sections on each of these.

Further, service blueprinting can be the basis of "service positioning" using the SERVQUAL dimensions (see separate section) of "RATER". Thus a service interaction can be designed using a blueprint to specifically emphasise Reliability (say by providing computer-based maintenance backup), Assurance (say by emphasising care and security), Tangibles (giving particular emphasis to on stage activities and visibles), Empathy (say by emphasising individual care), and Responsiveness (say by providing extra capacity to enable staff to be flexible).

"Service Odysseys"

In tourism, it has been suggested by Gyimothy, vistors tend to see the whole "package" rather than individual MoTs. She suggests four categories, "Great Explorer" (who like to explore and have a scout spirit), "Vagabonds" (who seek real life experiences), "Grand Tourists" (the travelling aristocrats), and "Colonists" (who claim and reconfirm their 'ownership'). Each category has different expectations and requirements. Grand Tourists expect perfect hotels and travel arrangements; "Explorers" seek opportunity; Vagabonds like local interaction and laid-back atmosphere; Colonists like good value but 'expect' some problems. Interesting implications.

Further reading :
G. Lynn Shostack, "Designing Services that Deliver", *Harvard Business Review*, Jan / Feb 1984, pp 133-139
G. Lynn Shostack, "Service Positioning Through Structural Change", *Journal of Marketing*, Vol 51, January 1987, pp 34-43
Jane Kingman Brundage, "Service Mapping : Gaining a Concrete Perspective on Service System Design", in Eberhard Scheuing and William Christopher (eds), *The Service Quality Handbook,* Amacom, New York, 1993, pages 148-163
Szilvia Gyimothy, Odysseys: Analysing Service Journeys from the Customer's Perspective, *Managing Service Quality*, V10, N6, 2000, pp389-396

Customer Loyalty

Loyalty and retention have become big issues in service and manufacturing as evidence has mounted that loyal customers buy more products and services over time and become ever more profitable. Witness the growth of loyalty cards during the 1990s. Loyal customers are less expensive to advertise to, are early adopters of new products and services, and tend to give an increasing share of their business to their preferred suppliers. Loyal customers are also the source of word of mouth advertising – highly effective and free! However, the concepts are not without their critics.

This section relates closely to the section on the Service Profit Chain. The S-P-C established many of the linkages. Fred Reichheld, probably *the* guru of loyalty, was a student of Earl Sasser at Harvard. The feedback loop that is suggested is: Quality Service leads to Customer Satisfaction leads to Loyal Customers leads to Retained Customers leads to Increased Profit leads to improved Loyalty leads to better quality service.

Reichheld, Sasser and others at Harvard established the principle of the lifetime value of a customer. The lifetime value can be estimated by multiplying the average spend per period by the estimated period of retention. To this can be added additional purchases and profits from referrals, and subtracting the savings made by advertising to established customers. By contrast, Reichheld suggests (1996:2) that not managing retention may lose a company 50% of its customer base in five years, so he proposes retention as being as important a measure as profit or ROI.

TARP, a Boston based consultancy, has produced a often-quoted set of findings. (Goodman). These are:

* Problems decrease customer loyalty by 15% to 30%.
* Most customers encountering problems do not complain – hence the importance of actively soliciting complaints, because many complainants tell their friends.
* Quality of service can affect loyalty – perhaps a 50% gain in some industries. Customers who are completely satisfied with the resolution of a problem exhibit no less and sometimes more loyalty. "Mollified" complainants, by contrast, are only slightly more loyal than dissatisfied complainants.
* Service can affect word-of-mouth behaviour. Customers who are dissatisfied tell twice as many people about their experiences as do satisfied customers.

Building on these findings, TARP has developed a detailed methodology for costing customer loyalty. Refer to the article.

Reichheld identifies three categories of loyalty – customer, employee, and investor. Loyal employees are increasingly seen as being necessary for loyal customers.

Zeithaml and Bitner suggest that there are four types of retention strategy. (1) Financial bonds, for example, loyalty cards, pricing, and bundling; (2) Social Bonds, built through building personal relationships – these are more common in professional services; (3) Customisation bonds, whereby the provider seeks to understand the detailed requirements of customers through anticipation and customer knowledge – for example books provided with customer logo; and (4) Structural bonds where the service is designed specifically for the customer – for example by joint investment and in the book example by incorporating the specific chapters required. These four levels may be seen as successive- (2) building on (1) for example.

In his most recent writing Reichheld (2001) suggests that to really win loyal customers requires very senior managers to "walk that talk". He proposes six principles (1) Preach what you practice – the leader must articulate his views as well as practice them. (2) Win-win: this is building loyalty by making sure that both the company and the customer wins – it's no win if you take advantage. (3) Be picky – choose the customers to work with, don't accept all for short term gains. (4) Keep it simple – decentralise and delegate real authority to make service decisions rapidly. (5) Reward the right results – make sure that loyalty is rewarded, not short term gains. (6) "Listen hard, talk straight". This is really a restatement of one of Stephen Covey's 7 principles – "seek first to understand not to be understood"

Is Loyalty worth pursuing for all customers?

Apparently not. Some financial institutions now differentiate customers on a Pareto (ABC) basis. "A" class customers are cultivated with great attention, but "C" class are just not worth the effort. Worse, attention on "terrorist" customers may divert attention from good prospects. Some institutions have actively tried to discourage some customers from running high transaction, low balance accounts. This may be sensible and pragmatic, but beware because a few C class customers may eventually turn into A class. Dimensions other than current return are necessary.

Loyalty and Satisfaction

The relationship between customer satisfaction and customer loyalty remains a hot topic in service quality. Two concepts will be summarised here.

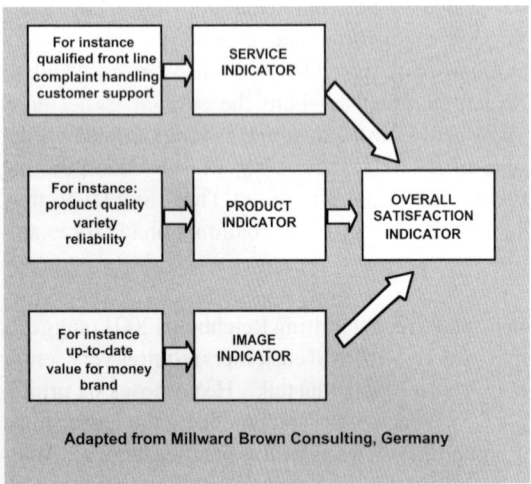

Adapted from Millward Brown Consulting, Germany

Millward Brown has suggested that an overall "satisfaction indicator" can be developed by combining several smaller indicators into one. Thus the task is to determine the quality dimensions that influence satisfaction. These are combined into area indicators which lead in turn to an overall service indicator or OSI. Three "area indicators" are Service, Product, and Image. His model is shown in the figure.

Neely, working with BA, has used a model similar to the "expectancy model" of motivation. Three types of antecedants: Cognitive (e.g. accessibility, confidence), Affective (e.g. emotions, feelings), and Conative (e.g. switching costs, expectations) together drive Attitudes and Patronage. These are also affected by norms and situational influences. Attitudes and Patronage in turn drive the loyalty consequences, which in turn feed back to the antecedants.

Thus prior circumstances that a customer knows or is aware of, combine with prior feelings and with earlier factors that require effort to change, to create an attitude relative to other competitors. These, however, are modified by actual events and norms to produce loyalty-related consequences. There is feedback at work.

The relationship between loyalty and satisfaction is seldom linear. Biemans suggests the following relationships for different industries:

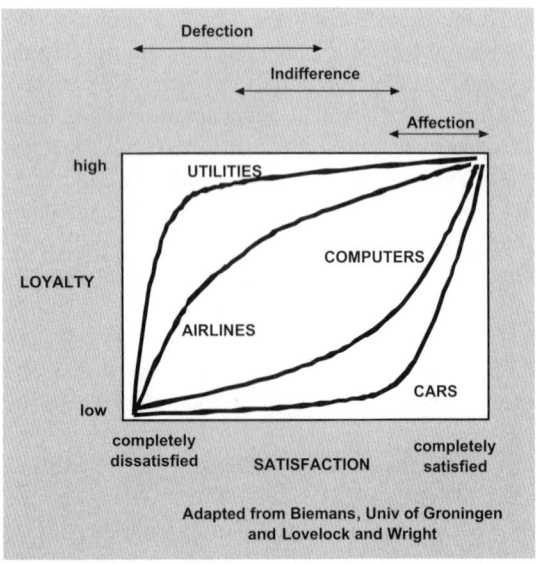

Adapted from Biemans, Univ of Groningen and Lovelock and Wright

The top lines indicate captive customers, so the bottom lines are more relevant. The shape indicates why for example Compac computer regards a satisfaction rating of 3.5 out of 5 as a failure.

On loyalty and repurchase, Stauss and Neuhaus suggest "five quality levels of satisfaction":

	Feeling	Repurchase
Demanding Satisfied	Optimism	Definitely
Stable Satisfied	Faith	Probably
Resigned Satisfied	Ignorance	Maybe
Stable Dissatisfied	Disappointment	Unlikely
Demanding Dissatisfied	Protest	No Way

After Stauss & Neuhaus, 1995

Complaint Handling

If TARP is to be believed managing complaints is important for retaining and even winning loyalty. Van Ossel and Stremersch suggest that complaints need to be handled rapidly but also that customers use three criteria: compensation, sincerity, and follow-up. Compensation is about fairness and can range from financial to replacement. Front-line staff may need special training in "sincerity" - real or perceived. And follow-up communication may be important with higher item services or purchases. It is the appropriate balance of all four which determines retention.

But beware, is much of this a myth? Henry warns of six common flaws about loyalty: (1) Retention is not the same as loyalty. (2) There may be many reasons for retention hiding under the heading of loyalty (geographically locked in, no alternative, switching costs, risk avoidance, other incentives such as frequent flyer schemes). (3) Profitability may be ascribed to loyalty when in fact superior business design drives both. (4) Managerial complacency. (5) Lifetime value is overstated. (6) A competitor's apparently loyal customers discourage effort.

Further reading

John Goodman, Pat O'Brien and Eden Segal, "Turning CFOs into Quality Champions", *Quality Progress*, March 2000, pp 47-54

Frederick Reichheld, *The Loyalty Effect*, Harvard Business School Press, 1996

Reichheld, F and Sasser, W., "Zero Defections: Quality Comes to Services", *Harvard Business Review*, Sept-Oct 1990, pp 105 – 111

Frederick Reichheld, "Lead for Loyalty", *Harvard Business Review*, July-August 2001, pp 76 – 84

Biemans, W. *Satisfaction vs. Loyalty*, Lecture Notes of University of Groningen, Holland, 2000

Stauss, B and Neuhaus, P quoted in Finn v.Hammerstein, *MScThesis*, University of Buckingham, 2000

Andy Neely, *Measuring Business Performance – Why, What and How*, The Economist Books, London, 1998

Millward Brown Consulting, Germany

Christopher Lovelock and Lauren Wright, *Principles of Service Marketing and Management*, Prentice Hall, New York, 1999

Craig Douglas Henry, "Is Customer Loyalty a Pernicious Myth?", *Business Horizons*, July-August 2000, pp 13-16

Gino Van Ossel and Stefan Stremersch, "Complaint Management", in Van Looy et al, *Services Management*, FT - Pitman, London, 1998

Please refer to the very closely related section on Service Recovery, Retention and the 3 R's.

Service Gaps, "SERVQUAL" and Service Dimensions

Zeithaml, Parasuraman and Berry (or PZB as they are sometimes known) have, over several years, developed a well researched and tested methodology for identifying the dimensions of service quality and the causes of "gaps" that exist between the service that customers expect and the perceived service that is received. The methodology is presented in detail in their book, which includes questionnaires that can often be used directly with customers. These have been widely used in service industry.

The author's set of five "dimensions of service quality" can be compared with David Garvin's dimensions - see under "The Gurus". Customers in service make up their mind about the quality of service by considering each of these five, although an individual customer would have his or her own preferences or weightings between them. The five are (1) "Tangibles", which includes the physical appearance of people equipment and facilities (2) "Reliability", which is to do with ability to perform the service dependably and accurately (i.e. doing what they say they will do, on time and to specification), (3) "Responsiveness", which concerns willingness to help and to respond to individual requirements, (4) "Assurance", which is the possession of the required knowledge, the skill to perform the service, and to convey trust, confidence, and security, (5) "Empathy" which begins with an understanding of the customer's needs and the ability to provide an individualised service. (These can be remembered by the mnemonic RATER). Taken together the five are known as "SERVQUAL", a registered phrase which is widely known. Like Garvin's dimensions, these form a very useful checklist. The authors have found, in a wide variety of surveys in different service sectors, where customers are asked to allocate 100 points between the five factors to indicate relative importance, that the Reliability dimension is the one which is most highly valued. The next two highest valued dimensions are Responsiveness and Assurance.

SERVQUAL helps identify customer perceptions of service quality. The 'gaps' analysis takes this further and helps identify the causes of service quality shortfalls in each or all of the dimensions. According to the authors, customers build an expectation of the service to be received depending on four factors. These are, firstly, word-of-mouth communications obtained from friends and acquaintances, secondly, personal needs, thirdly, past experience and, lastly, communications put out by the service company which create their own expectations. The authors refer to "Gap 5" as being the difference between expected service and the perceived service experienced. Gap 5 is the "customer gap" Gap 5 results from a combination of Gaps 1 to 4 (the "provider gaps"). These are :

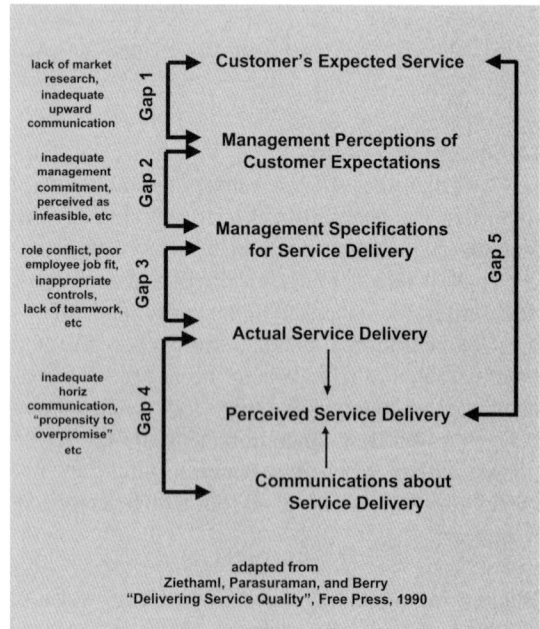

Gap 1 results from a difference between what customers expect and what management perceives these expectations to be. This can occur, for example, as a result of management not undertaking sufficient research or from communication failures within the company

Gap 2 results from a difference between management perceptions of what customers expect and the specifications that management draws up, or fails to draw up, spelling out what service quality delivery actions are required. This can result from inadequate management commitment and interest, from a perception that the company cannot actually meet customer requirements, from a failure to specify in detail what is required, or from a failure in the way in which the company sets its goals in relation to customers.

Gap 3 results from a mismatch between the service delivery specifications required by management and the actual service that is delivered by front line staff. There are many possible causes of this gap. Some include inappropriate technology, inappropriate staff or training, poor teamwork, and inappropriate control measures and methods. Gap 3 requires appropriate standards to be in place.

Finally Gap 4 results from a difference between the actual service that is delivered and messages that are put out to customers about what to expect. Clearly a major reason for this is poor internal communication and lack of familiarity with operations. There is also the often-found "propensity to overpromise". Clearly it is more desirable to under-promise and over-deliver.

Zeithaml and Bitner have written a whole text book around the closing of these gaps. Thus to close the customer gap requires all four provider gaps to be closed. So service quality, as we have heard before, begins with understanding customer expectations. These are "situational" - they vary by circumstance.

The fact that, under SERVQUAL, service quality is determined by the overall gap between what was expected and what was delivered, is important. It means that service quality is relative not absolute, and that different customers may perceive the level of service quality differently; that quality is determined by the customer who has "all the votes", not by the service provider; that service quality can be achieved by either meeting or exceeding expectations (see the Kano model), or by changing expectations (Gap 4, above).

Recent work has shown that the SERVQUAL dimensions and weightings do not necessarily apply in all parts of the world. For instance, Far East airline passengers seem to value respect above reliability.

Finland's Christian Grönroos views service quality as having 6 dimensions, the first four of which are roughly in line with those of PZB. These are Professionalism and Skills (assurance), Attitudes and Behaviour (empathy), Accessibility and Flexibility (responsiveness), and Reliability and Trustworthiness (reliability). Grönroos' additional two factors are Recovery and Problem Solving (the importance of which has been stressed by Reichheld and Sasser in their work on customer retention (see separate section), and Reputation and Credibility (to do with the image of the business in the mind of the customer, which overlaps with the concept of capability by Heskett, Sasser and Schlesinger (see the section on The Service Profit Chain).

Bienstock et al have suggested that the dimensions of timeliness, availability, and condition are also important dimensions in physical distribution and transport services.

Further reading
Valerie Zeithaml, A. Parasuraman, and Leonard Berry, *Delivering Quality Service*, Free Press, New York,1990.
Dick Schaaf, *Keeping the Edge : Giving Customers the Service They Demand*, Plume Penguin, New York, 1997, Part 2.
Valirie Zeithaml and Mary Jo Bitner, *Services Marketing*, Second edition, McGraw Hill, New York, 2000
Bienstock, Mentzer, and Bird, "Measuring Physical Distribution Service Quality", *Jnl Academy of Marketing Science*, V25, N1, 1997

The Service Profit Chain

The Service Profit Chain is a series of concepts developed by Heskett, Sasser and Schlesinger following years of research at Harvard Business School. It provides the foundation for work on Loyalty (see separate section). To quote the authors: "Service profit chain thinking maintains that there are direct and strong relationships between profit, growth, customer loyalty, customer satisfaction, the value of goods and services delivered to customers; and employee capability, satisfaction, loyalty, and productivity." In other words this is a systems approach to service quality, maintaining that there are a host of interacting factors and feedback loops at work. The book on the topic is a "tour de force" on service quality, with much relevance for manufacturing also.

The service profit chain model has been adapted by several others including the EFQM model and the Chris Voss studies. See the section on EFQM.

A central feature of the Service Profit Chain model is an equation for customer value which is

$$\text{Customer Value} = \frac{\text{Results} + \text{Process Quality}}{\text{Price} + \text{Customer Access Costs}}$$

In other words service quality includes both hard and soft factors, but is modified by price and influenced by ease of access. "Results" reminds us that customers buy benefits, not products or services. "Process Quality" is various service dimensions such as the RATER dimensions discussed under SERVQUAL. "Access" is to do with convenience in time and place of acquiring the service.

The service profit chain establishes the links between internal employee factors (loyalty, satisfaction, capability, service quality) which impact productivity and output quality. Variables here are factors such as workplace design, job design, selection, development, rewards, recognition, information and communication, and adequate "tools". Productivity and output quality impact value. Value impacts Customer satisfaction. Satisfaction impacts loyalty.

Loyalty impacts revenue and profitability.

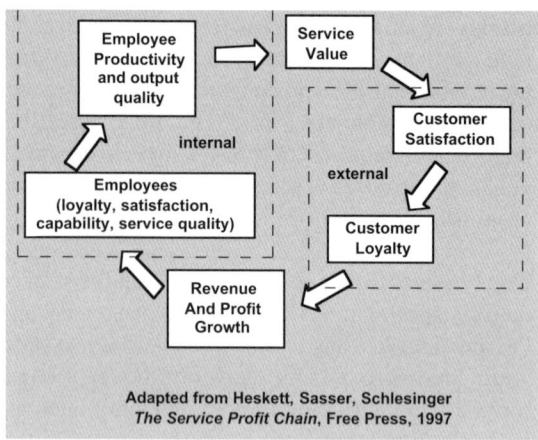

Adapted from Heskett, Sasser, Schlesinger
The Service Profit Chain, Free Press, 1997

On the customer side, the authors have identified and established links between the elements of the profit chain, as shown in the figure. Many of the linkages shown have been researched amongst leading companies, but much remains to be done. The service profit chain therefore provides a useful and interesting framework both for managers and for academic research. As such it is a very comprehensive work, the relevance of which can only grow.

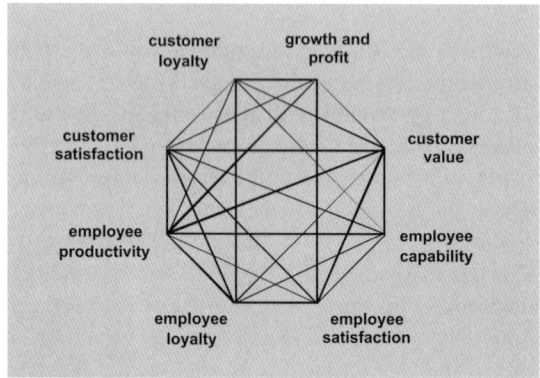

Further reading

James Heskett, W Earl Sasser, Leonard Schlesinger, *The Service Profit Chain*, The Free Press, New York, 1997

Service Recovery, Customer Retention and the "Three R's"

Two significant pieces of research are highlighted in this section which, when combined, have great significance for customer retention in service business.

The first is a study by Reichheld and Sasser. These researchers reported the powerful impact of customer defections on the "bottom line". Several cases are quoted. (For example in a credit card company, priority was given to gathering information from defecting customers, adjusting products and services accordingly. As a result profits increased sixteen fold without acquisitions). Retained customers generate increasing profits the longer they stay : setup costs are paid, advertising costs decline, and prices may be increased. One rule of thumb is that it costs 5 times as much to acquire a new customer as it does to retain an existing one. As a result, Reichheld and Sasser maintain that customer retention is a more important determinant of profitability than market share.

The second is work by Technical Assistance Research Programs, Inc. a U.S. based research organisation which has produced some widely quoted, and very significant, findings which are especially important to service quality in general and "service recovery" (i.e. recovering from poor service delivery) in particular.

In response to the Question "How many of your unhappy customers will buy other products or services offered by your company?", TARP found that, for small and medium purchases:

* approximately 85% of customers who had experienced no problem would repurchase.
* only around 45% of customers who are dissatisfied and who complain, would repurchase.
* but, where the complaint is "mollified" the repurchase percentage rises to around 80%,
* and, where the complainant is satisfied, the percentage exceeds 90% (i.e. above the percentage who experienced no problem!).

TARP also found (U.S. figures) that only a small percentage of dissatisfied customers (perhaps 20%) actually complain, but even less (perhaps 4%) go to the trouble to write. The point is that many front line complaints are lost though employees not passing on the information. Worse though is the finding that dissatisfied customers do not complain to the company, but nevertheless tell an average of 9 to 10 other people. TARP also found that approximately one third of complaints relate to problems caused by customers themselves (for example, unclear instructions).

Customer retention should therefore be a high priority. Ways to go about this include the following:

* "Watching the Door", or identifying customers who have just "defected" or who are about to leave. Sometimes this can be easy where there are established accounts which have become non-operative (or even where use has declined significantly), but may be more difficult where customers are nameless as in retailing. Here loyalty schemes such as store cards may be an answer. An efficient feedback process as to the reasons for defections is required. Of course, it should be kept up to date.
* Making complaining easier. Passive customer survey information collection is routinely attempted at hotels, but ways need to be found to make this more active by, for example, rewards. In any case have free phone or reply paid mail.
* A "no quibble" policy on returns.
* Key account management, including careful and regular monitoring.
* Trying to stay ahead of the game by identifying future expectations. One way is to work through so called "lead users" - the innovators who buy early.
* Eliminating any "climate of fear" as Deming would have called it, which prevents onward communication of poor performance. An attitude that a dissatisfied customer is an opportunity not a threat needs to pervade an organisation, but is especially important for first tier managers.

* Offer some compensation, even if small : a voucher or free meal. In Britain "service guarantees" are offered by telephone and water companies.
* Have a preplanned service recovery process : recognise that some service failures are predicable, others not, but that a routine should be worked out for the former category. This routine swings into place automatically when service failure occurs. Of course, such routines should not prevent seeking a failsafe solution.
* Explain what happened to the customer. TARP research suggests that a clear explanation is more effective than just fixing the problem.
* Giving employees the authority to solve customer problems right there and then; don't add to the problem by shifting responsibility.

Heskett, Sasser and Schlesinger have therefore proposed an extension to the traditional 4 P's of marketing (Product, Price, Place, Promotion), as being more appropriate to the service firm (but, no doubt, also very relevant to manufacturing firms that invariably bundle product and service). These are the Three R's : Retention, Referrals, and Related Products. Retention is the ability to hold on to valuable customers (whilst also identifying and dropping low loyalty, very dissatisfied customers - whom these authors refer to as "terrorists"). Referrals is the ability to gain from word of mouth recommendations - which are not only free but the have the highest credibility. And selling related products and services is made easier and more cost effective by the reputation for value and customer care from loyal customers.

On retention, loyalty and referrals, the final word goes to Marge Simpson who said, "Dear God, if you save us from the tornado I will be very grateful and will recommend you to all my friends."

Further readings:
Frederick Reichheld and W Earl Sasser Jr., "Zero Defections : Quality Comes to Services", *Harvard Business Review*, Vol 70, Sept./October 1990, pages 105-111.
Frederick Reichheld, *The Loyalty Effect*, Harvard Business School Press, Boston, 1996.
Technical Assistance Research Programs, *Consumer Complaint Handling in America : an Update Study*, U.S. Office of Consumer Affairs, March 1986.
Valerie Zeithaml and Mary Jo Bitner, *Services Marketing*, Mc Graw Hill, New York, 1996, Chapters 6 and 16.
James Heskett, W Earl Sasser, Leonard Schlesinger, *The Service Profit Chain*, The Free Press, New York, 1997

Zone of Tolerance

Statistical Process Control thinking has been extended into the service area by, amongst others, Berry, Zeithaml and Bitner and by Johnston and Clark. Both refer to a zone of customer tolerance of customer satisfaction located between zones of delight and dissatisfaction. Berry's zone of tolerance falls between zones of desired service and adequate service, so perhaps is more like "Pre Control" than SPC. These conceptual models are useful in thinking about the bounds of service quality.

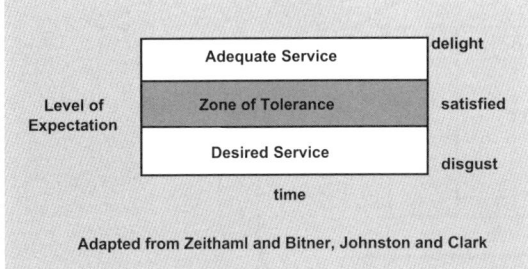

Adapted from Zeithaml and Bitner, Johnston and Clark

Both sets of authors make the point that the zone can shift depending on the importance of the factor and upon prior experience. Thus the zone is wider for first time buyers but narrows for service recovery situations. The size of the band may also be affected by the level of interest and commitment.

Johnston and Clark use the Zone of Tolerance concept much like an SPC control chart, maintaining that various "transactions" or moments of truth can be plotted in the chart. A succession of points plotted in the dissatisfied zone leads to the equivalent of out of control conditions (a dissatisfied customer) but several points above the zone result in delight. Presumably the SPC "out of control" apply - one very high (unsatisfactory) point or several successive more or less unsatisfactory points would both lead to an "out of control" condition (in SPC language). Some behaviour may be compensatory – a poor experience may be compensated by several satisfactory experiences. A poor experience may also shift the 'control limits' upwards making the customer even more demanding, but a great experience may lower the zone thus making it easier to achieve further delight.

A great experience may lower the tolerances for subsequent events.

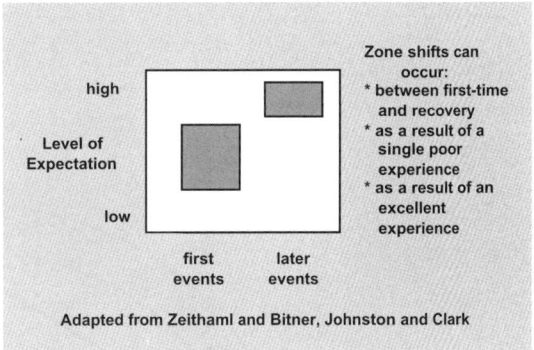

Adapted from Zeithaml and Bitner, Johnston and Clark

Zeithaml and Bitner have done interesting work identifying the factors that shift the control limits (although they don't use these terms). The upper limit of the zone (leading to desired service) is influenced by implicit and explicit service promises, by word of mouth and by past experience. The lower limit is influenced by:

* "service intensifiers" (where, for example, an anniversary dinner might imply reduced tolerance)
* by service alternatives (where there are fewer options there is more tolerance)
* the degree of influence that a customer has on the service provider
* factors that are perceived to be out of the service provider's control.
* the predicted service.

Although conceptual in nature, these are useful ideas particularly when used with service mapping, moments of truth, and the Kano model (See section on Service Blueprinting). Thus Kano Delighters more or less correspond to Adequate Service zone, and Performance factors to the Zone of Tolerance.

Further reading
Valerie Zeithaml and Mary Jo Bitner, *Services Marketing*, McGraw Hill, Boston, 2000, Chapter 3
Leonard Berry, *Marketing Services: Competing through Quality*, Free Press, New York, 1991
Robert Johnston and Graham Clark, *Service Operations Management*, FT/Prentice Hall, Harlow, 2000, Chapter 4

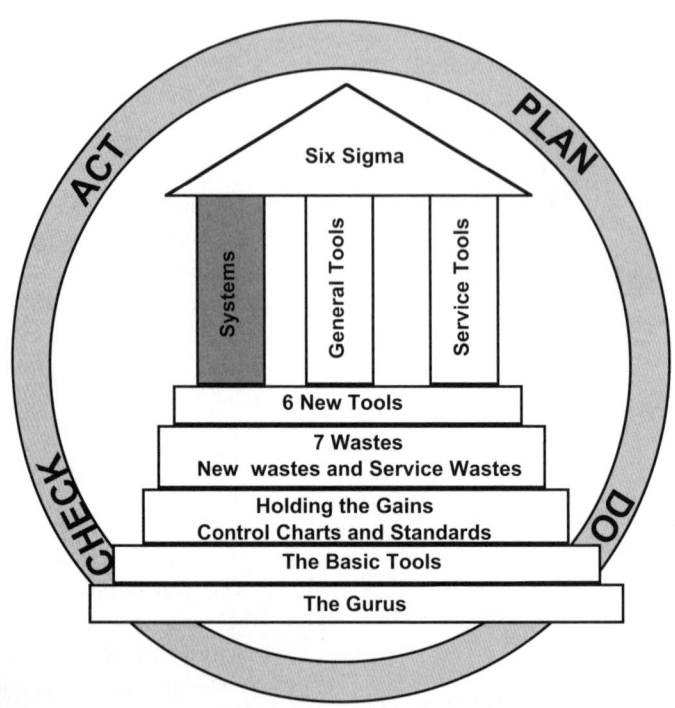

Systems

**ISO 9001:2000
EFQM Excellence Model**

ISO 9001:2000

ISO 9001:2000 is the new international standard on quality assurance, applicable to manufacturing and service. The new standard was published in December 2000. The previous version had accumulated some 350k registrations in 150 countries by January 2000. The 2000 version represents a considerable advance on the previous 1994 version which set down 20 clauses that organisations seeking accreditation had to demonstrate. ISO 9001 can be used by an organisation to both *demonstrate* its ability and to *assess* its ability to meet customer requirements. ISO 9001 sets the quality system standards, not the product standards. Quality is defined as the "degree to which a set of inherent characteristics fulfils requirements."

The 2000 version is based on eight Quality Management Principles that are an excellent guide to modern thinking on quality. The principles are:

* *Customer Focused Organisation*. It is customers, not the organisation that defines quality, so look outward rather than inward. Survival ultimately depends upon understanding customer needs.
* *Leadership* – is necessary to drive the organisation to meet customer needs and to improve.
* *Involvement of People*. It is the people in the organisation that makes for high quality products and services.
* *Process Approach*. It is linked (horizontal) processes, transforming inputs into outputs, which produce the requirements of customers. It is not functional departments or (vertical) 'silos'. (This is perhaps the most fundamental change to the previous standard which emphasised the responsibilities of functions). The continuous improvement process involves establishing objectives (a management responsibility), resource management, realising the product or service, and measurement and analysis.
* *Systems Approach:* The organisation is a system: it has inputs, outputs, information flows, goals, controls, and interactions. Processes come together to form purposeful systems.
* *Continual Improvement* – is necessary for survival. Everyone needs to participate. (This links with Kaizen)
* *Fact-based Approach*. As Deming said, 'In God we trust; all others must bring data". (This links with "Gemba")
* *Supplier Relationships*. A well known and valid saying is that 'companies don't compete, supply chains compete'. Ultimately quality depends upon the company and its suppliers.

The new standard has core sections which are broadly similar to the Deming PDCA cycle. Management must plan the system in relation to customers, the resources must be provided, the activities carried out, and then measured, analysed and improved. The standard provides fairly specific guidelines and advice on each. In the overview below, some important points are highlighted. For people not involved in quality certification, it is instructive to read through the following section to gain an impression of an integrated view of quality.

* *General Requirements*. Like the previous version, the phrase "say what you do and do what you say" still applies. You make up the rules for your own organisation following the guidelines. Then you are expected to follow them and be audited upon them. The organisation must identify the necessary processes, determine criteria, ensure the availability of resources, monitor and measure, and implement to achieve results and continual improvement. (In short, PDCA).
* *Management Responsibility*. Management must establish the quality policy, the policy must be communicated, and management must demonstrate and give evidence of its commitment. Senior management must ensure that customer needs and expectations are determined, and ensure that the organisation is able to fulfil the requirements. Processes must be identified. A quality management system must be established, documented, maintained, and improved. A management representative must promote an awareness of customer requirements. And a review process must take place to ensure that the quality

system remains effective.

* *Resource Management.* This covers human resources, facilities, and the work environment. Management must determine and provide the necessary resources and facilities to implement the system and to address customer satisfaction. Records must be kept of experience, training, and qualifications. Training must be evaluated.

* *Product (or Service) Realisation.* This is a mini PDCA cycle within the broader quality system. The emphasis is on process. The steps of the process must be determined, say by flowcharts. Customer requirements must be clearly understood and orders not accepted until there is the ability to meet the requirements. Communication with the customer must take place. The process must be designed, reviewed, verified, and measured, all in relation to the customer. ISO requires a system for suppliers to be identified, selected, communicated with, and evaluated. Then the entire process needs to be controlled by having acceptance criteria, work standards, capable processes, and procedures for release, delivery and service. ISO also gives guidelines on traceability, customer property, preservation of product, process validation (for example SPC), and the control of measuring devices

* *Design and Development.* These requirements ensure that the process of design is planned and controlled. The organisation is expected to design the stages, review and validate, and clarify responsibilities.

* *Purchasing and Production and Service Provision.* Purchased product must conform to requirements and suppliers must be chosen and evaluated in relation to criteria that must be established. Production must be carried out under controlled conditions, including work standards, equipment, and monitoring and measurement. In short using standard operations and capable equipment.

* *Measurement, Analysis, Improvement.* Finally the system needs to be measured, monitored and controlled, and improved. Non-conformities need to be controlled. The new standard is more specific on improvement and on customer satisfaction which needs to be included in any performance measurement system. Processes and products need to be monitored. Importantly feedback needs to be given to Management Review thereby closing the loop.

ISO 9001 includes reduced requirements for documentation in comparison with the old standard. The organisation has greater freedom to specify its own documentation, but must nevertheless have documentation for the effective planning, operation and control of its processes. Six types of documentation are specifically required. For: control of documents, control of nonconforming products, corrective actions, preventive actions, control of records, and for internal quality audits.

Criticisms of the old standard cited its cost to implement, excessive "red tape", its unsuitability for particular kinds of industry (witness the emergence of the auto industry standard QS9000), and the possibility of management attention being diverted from real quality issues. On the positive side certification gives credibility, a reduction in the necessity for supplier audits, and may bring order to an undisciplined company. Hopefully the problems have been reduced, whilst benefits remain.

Further reading and Notes

ISO 9001:2000 Quality Management Systems: Requirements. This is the standard for demonstrating conformity of a quality management system.

ISO 9004:2000. Guidelines for performance improvement. This is not for certification purposes but provides guidelines for both meeting customer requirements and improving performance.

ISO 9000:2000. This discusses the fundamental concepts and sets out definitions.

Charles Cianfrani, Joseph Tsiakals, John West, *ISO 9001:2000 Explained.* (Second edition), ASQ Quality Press, Milwaukee, 2001. This book contains the entire standard.

Web site: www.bsi.org.uk

The Quality Certification Bureau at www.qcbinc.com provides several comprehensive implementation and assessment guides on the standard which can be downloaded.

EFQM Excellence Model (and other models)

A European equivalent was started by the European Foundation for Quality Management (EFQM) in 1992. This is known as the Business Excellence Model. This is a "non-prescriptive framework which recognises there are many approaches to achieving sustainable excellence". It is a self-evaluation tool for organisations, large and small, public and private sector. The EFQM updates the model regularly. The model is shown in the Figure. Each of the nine boxes has sub-criteria for which there are a number of questions. Below each sub-criterion are lists of areas to consider. A full set of evaluation criteria is available from the EFQM website.

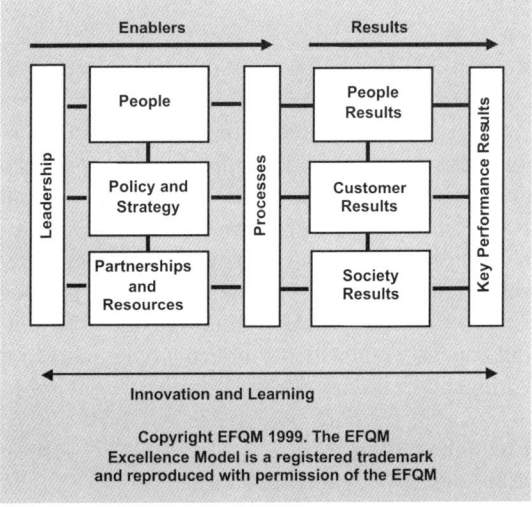

Copyright EFQM 1999. The EFQM Excellence Model is a registered trademark and reproduced with permission of the EFQM

The introductory section of this book gives the quality tools that may be relevant to each of the nine boxes of the EFQM model.

Some brief comments on the nine boxes follow:
Leadership
The importance of leadership is recognised, as is establishing vision and mission. EFQM defines leaders in wide terms, not limited to top management. Leaders are expected to be role models, and to improve their own performance. PDCA is not just for products and processes! EFQM is very much a Deming viewpoint on leadership ("constancy of purpose").
People
EFQM covers such "obvious" aspects as training and evaluation, but goes further requiring effective human resource development, teamworking, empowerment, and rewards and recognition.
Policy and Strategy
The EFQM is concerned not just with product and service quality, however important, but also with organisational policy and strategy. The "stakeholder" concept is used, and EFQM would expect a balanced consideration of all stakeholders. Policy deployment, to ensure that strategy is communicated, is important.
Partnerships and Resources
Active encouragement of supplier partnerships is given, with emphasis on mutually beneficial relationships. Interestingly EFQM talks about the use and development of knowledge. On resources, of course facilities need to be maintained for capability, but there is also mention of conservation of materials.
Processes
The focus of EFQM is on the key processes necessary to deliver the organisation's strategy. Of course quality processes are also important, such as Kaizen initiatives, and ISO 9001. Again a Deming viewpoint ("management by facts").
People Results
People are supposed to be adequately surveyed, with ideas such as team briefings and suggestion schemes incorporated.
Customer Results
This major box requires evaluation of customer satisfaction through surveys and interviews. Loyalty and market share are measures.
Society Results
EFQM asks the company to establish its impact on wider society, for example involvement in community activities.
Key Performance Results
EFQM requires a "balanced scorecard" type approach, as well as cost of quality, product and process measures.

It may be seen that EFQM goes well beyond a narrow

definition of Quality. Perhaps what Juran would call "Big Q"?

EFQM and ISO 9001:2000.
Having said that EFQM interprets quality in a far wider sense, there are similarities and overlaps between the two. "Fundamental Concepts" underpin the EFQM model. These are broadly in line with the eight principles of ISO 9001, but with a much broader interpretation by EFQM in each case. The EFQM concepts are, with the corresponding ISO principle shown in brackets:

Results orientation   (   )
Customer focus   (Customer focus)
Leadership and constancy of purpose
                            (Leadership)
Management by Process and Facts
            (Process Approach)(Factual approach)
People development and involvement
                            (Involvement of people)
Continuous learning, innovation, improvement
                            (Continual improvement)
Partnership development
            (Mutually beneficial supplier development)
Public responsibility   (   )
———   (System approach to management)

There are also similarities with the Service Profit Chain Model.

Service Excellence, Drivers, and Complacency

On business excellence, Chris Voss et al at London Business School undertook a survey of UK and US businesses. This used criteria based on the EFQM and on several other models. (It is possible to survey and benchmark your own organisation using these criteria via "Service Probe" marketed by the CBI, London – unfortunately not free like others).
Some interesting findings were

* There is a good correlation between what the authors termed "Results" (market share, profit, customer and staff satisfaction) and "Drivers" (including process orientation, employees, measures, organisation structure)
* In the UK there is a smaller proportion of "World Class" service companies than in the USA but the USA has a higher percentage of "laggards"
* The "world class" companies tend to be much less complacent than the "laggards". In other words managers who regarded themselves as well above were often below average, and those who believe that they still have much to learn generally have above average results. (It's something to do with the Deming Cycle and the failure to check and learn!)

The Drivers that Voss et al use are in some ways similar to the Enablers in the Business Excellence model.

Robson and Prabhu have used the Voss model to study the performance of a large number of northern British service companies. They identify the following factors as being good predictors of performance attainment: Strategy towards corporate and social responsibility, employee loyalty, staff responsiveness, customer satisfaction as well as market share, cash flow and costs. Predictors for good practice adoption include benchmarking, skill and job training, customer orientation, problem solving, and waste elimination.

Further reading
Web sites: www.efqm.org
Chris Voss, Kate Blackmon, Richard Chase et al, *Achieving World-Class Service*, London Business School, 1997.
Andrew Robson and Vas Prabhu, "What can we learn from leading service practitioners...", *Managing Service Quality*, V11, N4, 2001

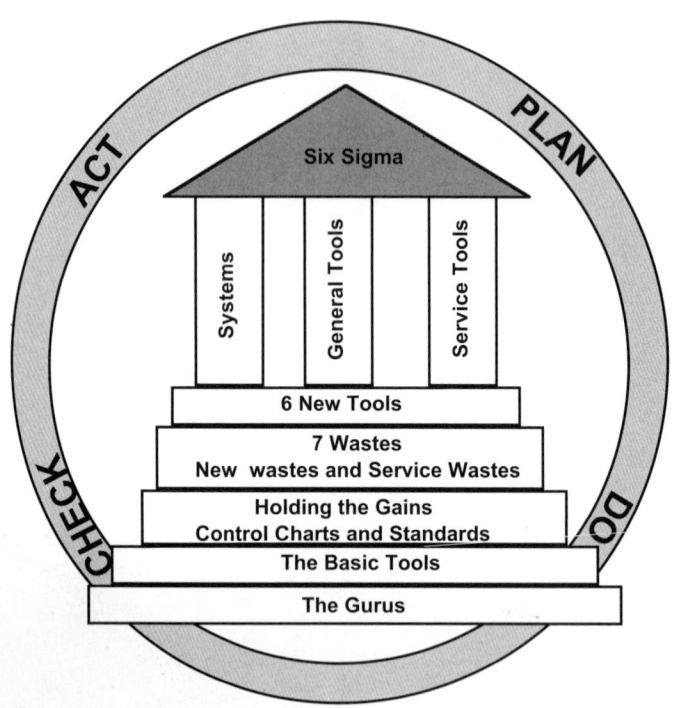

Six Sigma

Six Sigma is a quality methodology, originating in Motorola in 1987 who called their approach "Six Sigma" when winning the 1998 Baldridge Award. There is little doubt that Six Sigma has taken over from TQM to emerge as the most significant development in Quality in recent years. It is now used widely in manufacturing and service. The methodology was given a boost in 1997 when Jack Welch of GE praised it in the annual company report, claiming $300m of savings. The term Six Sigma indicates its strong relationship to statistics, measurement and variation although it would be a mistake to bound it in this narrow way. "Sigma" is the recognised symbol for one standard deviation.

The term "six sigma" derives from the spread of the normal distribution (plus and minus 3 standard deviations or 3 sigma indicating the control limits). If specification limits can be set and the process spread limited such that the distance from the process centre line to the nearest specification limit is six standard deviations, then a highly capable process will have been achieved. Even if the process were to shift by 1.5 sigma, the risk of producing defects would still be limited to 3.4 parts per million (There would still be 1.5 standard deviations from the control limit to the nearest specification limit - this topic is developed further in the section on Capability). So "six sigma performance" means close to perfection. Thus short term performance might achieve a Cpk of 2 but with process drift over the medium term Cpk may decline to 1.5

Whether or not a process can achieve 3.4 defects per million, is in a sense not the point. The point is the rigorous process that moves one towards the goal. It is probably true that today most manufacturing firms are achieving 3 or 4 sigma performance (6210 ppm is 4 sigma), and most service firms achieve around 2 sigma (309,000 ppm). Six Sigma also uses DPMO (defects per million opportunities) sometimes in preference to ppm. See the separate section on this topic, and the table on the next page.

Six Sigma is also concerned not only with reducing the number of defects but also with reducing the variation or spread. Part (or product) variation and Process variation are both of concern. In the figure below loan approval time is the attribute most important to the customer. Six Sigma would aim not only to reduce the number of applications that are not dealt with in the specified time, but also to reduce the spread of approval times. Thereafter the target time could be reduced to form a new goal.

Six Sigma uses a standardised improvement cycle based on the Deming PDCA cycle, known as DMAIC (define, measure, analyse, improve, control). See the separate section on PDCA and DMAIC. So, in the figure, first measure the distribution of loan approval times. Then, using DMAIC, try to move the distribution to the left but also try to narrow the distribution. Most of the tools in this book constitute the basic Six Sigma toolbox. They need to be used in an organised sequence. See the figure on PDCA and DMAIC given at the beginning of this book which list the tools for each stage.

SIX SIGMA: CORE CONCEPTS

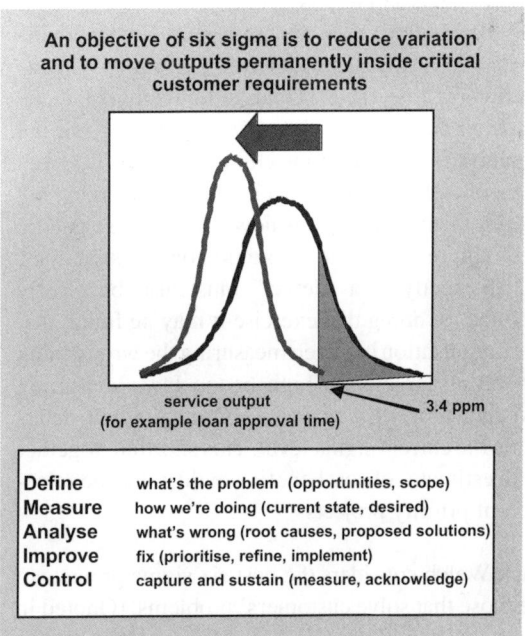

Is Six Sigma merely total quality management (TQM) in different clothing? Certainly not. Six Sigma is far more "hard nosed", putting emphasis on driving results to the bottom line. It is far more data-based than TQM that in some companies was little more than an ill defined motivation or culture programme. It uses a defect measure to track performance. It uses Juran's concept of project-by-project improvement. Thus Breyfogle uses the "S^4" approach which involves cyclic stages of Strategy, Training, Project Management, Audit and back to Strategy all making use of appropriate tools.

A starting point is the belief in process. An organisation is characterised by processes, frequently cross-functional. A process has inputs. It also has outputs that can be measured, directly or indirectly. A process can be mapped. Suppliers, process, and customers all require focus.

Six Sigma uses the concept of "critical to quality" (CTQ) characteristics. CTQ characteristics are those most important to the customer, and it is these that need to be clearly specified and measured. Vital tasks are therefore to determine specific customer requirements and to convert them into CTQ metrics and distributions. See the section on customer surveys. This also ties in with Hoshin activities - see the section on this. The CTQ target limits must then be set *from the point of view of the customer*, not the organisation. It is often useful to look at CTQ from the pont of view of a decision tree whereby big requirements are broken down into more specific sub-requirements. See the section on decision trees. What exactly is a "defect" must also be clearly defined. In doing this exercise it may be found that the organisation has been measuring the wrong thing or setting targets too high or too low. Measuring existing processes against CTQ targets will determine the current sigma level. This shortfall, together with estimates of cost benefit, would guide the selection of priority projects

Jack Welch considers the best six sigma projects to be those that solve customers' problems. (Quoted in *Jack Welch and the GE Way*, McGraw Hill, 1999).

No doubt what attracted Jack Welch to Six Sigma is its hard-nosed approach to the bottom line. Six Sigma projects are supposed to generate bottom line cash savings, project by project. Process measures are taken before and after. Hence the importance of Cost of Quality concepts (see the separate section on CoQ) and on ppm and DPMO.

SIX SIGMA PERFORMANCE

Sigma Level	ppm (1.5 sigma shifted)
1	697672
2	308770
3	66810
4	6209
5	232
6	3.4

GE's version of Six Sigma revolves around six key principles. These are an interesting "slant" on the views used in this book.
Critical to Quality. The starting point is the customer, and those attributes most important to the customer must be determined.
Defect. A defect is anything that fails to deliver exactly what the customer requires.
Process Capability. Processes must be made capable of delivering customer requirements.
Variation. As experienced by the customer. What the customer sees and feels.
Stable Operations. The aim is to ensure consistent, predictable processes to improve the customer's experience.
Design for Six Sigma. Design must meet customer needs and process capability.

Pande et al give six themes of Six Sigma. (Comments are added by the author) (1) A genuine focus on the customer. (Unlike TQM which was full of good intentions, but often remote from specific customer objectives. Both Six Sigma and Lean begin with the customer.) (2) Data and fact driven management (As Deming famously said, "In God we trust. All others must bring data.") (3) Process focus and improvement. (Process was also central in TQM. In six sigma DMAIC improvement is at the core.) (4) Proactive.

(Six Sigma tries to anticipate problems, not merely solve them). (5) Boundaryless collaboration. (Six Sigma teams and projects work cross functionally to improve processes.) (6) Six Sigma seeks perfection but takes risks. (In other words risk is inherent if one wants to 'breakthrough' to ever higher levels of improvement. See Blitz and Disruptive Technology.)

Six Sigma is usually driven by people qualified in the methodology, rather than by people from HR which was frequently the case with TQM. A useful innovation has been to recognise Six Sigma expertise by judo-type belts. A black belt typically requires four weeks of training held over four months and requires practical results. The four weeks correspond to Measure, Analyse, Improve, Control in the DMAIC cycle. Black belts often work full time on Six Sigma projects and typically aim at savings exceeding $200k per year. Master black belts are more experienced black belts who act as mentors. There are also Six Sigma "Champions" who define the WHAT (a very important role, requiring cross functional and cross process knowledge), whereas Black Belts are concerned with the HOW. Some companies retain their Black Belts for between two and three years, and thereafter move them into line management positions or Champion positions. Green belts go through less rigorous training. Some companies, for instance Allied Signal / Honeywell have set goals of 90% of the workforce becoming green belts within 5 years. In a Six Sigma project there is typically a process owner, team leaders, a black belt, perhaps several green belts, and team members.

So called Design for Six Sigma (DFSS) addresses design of product and process issues. This final step is very often necessary to move from four or five sigma to six sigma performance. Design robustness is a major concern. Taguchi methods, tolerancing, and QFD are typical required skills. In DFSS we talk about Define, Measure, Analyse, Design, and Verify rather than DMAIC.

Implementation and human issues are considered to be as important as the six sigma tools themselves. Some implementation tools are given in this book – see the DMAIC section, and the sustainability section.

Lean and Six Sigma
Of late Six Sigma has joined up with other improvement approaches, especially Lean Thinking. The Maytag Corporation, for instance, has called their joint approach "LeanSigma" and registered this name as a service mark. These two methodologies work synergistically together. Both aim at reducing waste and variation. Both encourage the concept of continuous improvement via a PDCA cycle or similar. Lean puts emphasis on the physical layout, on standardisation and 5S, on one-piece flow in cells and on lead time reduction. Six Sigma on the other hand provides a powerful methodology for measurement, problem solving, and control. As lean implementation proceeds, quality improves through better visibility, reduced number of process steps and "enforced" problem solving. As six sigma proceeds, flow is improved through reduced variation. Both ultimately benefit the customer.

Further reading
Forrest W Breyfogle III, *Implementing Six Sigma*, Wiley, New York, 1999 (for the techniques).
Forrest W Breyfogle, James Cupello, Becki Meadows, *Managing Six Sigma*, Wiley, New York, 2001. A management overview.
Peter Pande et al, *The Six Sigma Way*, McGraw Hill, New York, 2000 (for six sigma management and measurement)
Quality Progress magazine has a regular column in Six Sigma and details of six sigma software, hardware, and consulting services.
John Bicheno, *The Lean Toolbox*, (Second edition), PICSIE Books, Buckingham, 2000. This can be regarded as a companion volume to any six sigma programme.
As an interesting background to Six Sigma, see Robert Slater, *The GE Way Fieldbook: Jack Welch's Battle Plan for Corporate Revolution*, 1999
Web sites:
www.ge.com
www.mot.com

Index

14 point plan	8, 12
3 R's of Service	109
5 Whys	61
5S	59
6 Honest Serving Men	62
7 Tools	29
7 Wastes	53
Affinity Diagram	45
After Action Review	25
Appraisal Costs	69
Bateman	95
Benchmarking	63
Best Demonstrated Practice	65
Bhote	22, 74, 87
Blitz	66
Blueprinting	101
Bottleneck	54
Box and Whisker	71
Brainstorming	68
Breyfogle	119
c chart	39
CANDO	59
Capability	41
Change	95
Check Sheets	34
Christensen	75
Common Causes	40
Contingency Chart	47
Control charts	37
Correlation	33
Cost of Quality (CoQ)	68
Cp	41
Cpk	42
CPO	99
Critical Path Analysis	50
Critical to Quality (CTQ)	120
Crosby	12
Cross Impact Analysis	34
Customer Processing Operation	99
Cusums	71
Cycle of Service	99
Data Display	71
Deadly diseases	9
Defects	55
Defects per Million	72
Deming	7, 14, 53
Deming cycle	25
Design of Experiments	73
Dimensions, Quality	16, 106
Disruptive Technologies	75
DMAIC cycle	26
DOE	73
DPMO	72
Energy	56
EPE (every part every)	53
Excellence Model	115
Failsafing	17
Failure Costs	68
Failure Modes and Effect Analysis	76
Feigenbaum	13
Fishbone Diagram	31
FMEA	76
Force Field Analysis	77
Ford	27
Garvin	16
Gemba (place of action)	29, 82
General tools	58
Grönroos	22, 101, 107
Hines	78, 94
Histogram	31, 71
Holding the Gains	37, 95
Hoshin	78
Importance Performance Matrix	80
Improvement Cycles	25
Inappropriate Processing	54
Interaction	74
Interrelationship Diagram	46
Is Is-Not Analysis	62
Ishikawa	14, 31
ISO 9001:2000	113
JIT	53
JITII	94
Johari Window	81
Johnston	100, 111
Jones, Dan	29, 42, 53, 94
Juran	9
Kaikaku	66
Kaizen	82, 102
Kano	20, 102, 111
Kepner Tregoe	62

Lean	53, 120
Loss Function	18
Loyalty	103
Mackle	83
Mahesh	99
Manhattan diagrams	72
Mapping	29, 99
Market Survey	84
Matrix Analysis	49, 88
Mean and Range charts	38
Measles Chart	31
Measures	72, 79, 80
Moments of Truth (MoT)	100
Multi Vari Chart	32
Network Diagram	46, 50
New Wastes	56
NGT	85
Nominal Group Technique	85
Numbered Histograms	71
Oakland	40, 79
OEE	59, 88
Out of control	40
Overproduction	53
p chart	39
Pareto analysis	30
PDCA	4, 9, 25, 37
Performance	80
Performance-Importance	80
PETS	88
Pictorial Affinity Diagram	45
Pokayoke	17
Policy Deployment	78
Precontrol	87
Prevention	12, 37
Prevention Costs	68
Process Capability	40
Process Mapping	29
Process Model	88
Project management	50
QFD	88
Quality at Source	17
Quality Function Deployment	88
Radar Chart	71
RATER Service Dimensions	106
Recovery	109
Reichheld	103, 105
Retention	109
Root Cause Analysis	61
RPN	76
Run Diagram	32
Service Gaps	106
Service Profit Chain	108
Service Tools	98
Service Wastes	56
SERVQUAL	106
Shainin	22
Shingo	17
Shostack	102
Single Point Lessons	92
Six New Tools	44
Six Sigma	4, 26, 72, 119
Slack, Nigel	80
SOP	42
Spaghetti diagrams	29, 54, 102
SPC	37
Standard and Davis	95
Standard Operating Procedure	42
Standards	42
Statistical Process Control	37
Stratification	33
Supplier Partnership	94
Sustainability	95
Systems	7, 112
Taguchi	18
Tally Chart	34
TARP	103, 105
Tend to Zero	71
Tim Wood	53
Tolerance	42, 111
Transporting	54
Treatments	73
Tree Diagram	47
Trilogy (Juran)	10
Unnecessary Inventory	55
Unnecessary Motion	55
Value	108
von Hammerstein	104
Waiting	54
Waste	51
Welch, Jack	120
Womack	29
Zeithaml	22, 106
Zone of Tolerance	111

Books, Games and Slides from PICSIE

Books

The Lean Toolbox   John Bicheno 2000   A4   203 pages (Third edition January 2003)

Written in a short snappy style this guide to the essentials of Lean operations includes sections on historical dates, philosophy, planning, design, analysis and mapping, improvement, production, Goldratt, quality, suppliers and distribution, people, measurement. Second edition. Second edition. Foreword by Dan Jones, co-author of *Lean Thinking*

Cause and Effect Lean   John Bicheno   2000   A5   88 pages

Using fishbone diagrams, this guide maps out the main tools, sub tools, and sub-sub tools of Lean, Six Sigma, and Supply Chain This booklet has been updated three times since 1991. Widely used. Several hundred unsolicited testimonials have been received.

How 2 take your company on the Journey towards Lean by Kate Mackle   early 2003

This is a highly practical set of guides written for shop-floor to middle management. An ideal companion to anyone doing Current State to Future State mapping.

Games

The Buckingham Lean Game. An ideal game to learn Lean manufacturing. Unlike other games this game includes several products, changeover, quality, and right size machines. Can be adapted to multiple environments.

The Buckingham Supply Chain Game and LEAP Game
These two bundled games are excellent simulations of both the distribution chain and the supply chain. The LEAP Game was developed at Cardiff Univ.

The Buckingham Heijunka Game
This game illustrates how to transform a "current state" into a "future sate" using Heijunka (level scheduling) principles.

Slides

Copies of figures from most books are available on Powerpoint via internet